Insiders, Outliers

The American Campus

Founded by Harold S. Wechsler

The books in the American Campus series explore recent developments and public policy issues in higher education in the United States. Topics of interest include access to college and college affordability; college retention, tenure, and academic freedom; campus labor; the expansion and evolution of administrative posts and salaries; the crisis in the humanities and the arts; the corporate university and for-profit colleges; online education; controversy in sport programs; and gender, ethnic, racial, religious, and class dynamics and diversity. Books feature scholarship from a variety of disciplines in the humanities and social sciences.

For a complete list of titles in the series, please see the last page of the book.

Insiders, Outliers

Centering Adult Student Writers at an HBCU

COLLIE FULFORD

Rutgers University Press

New Brunswick, Camden, and Newark, New Jersey

London and Oxford

Rutgers University Press is a department of Rutgers, The State University of New Jersey, one of the leading public research universities in the nation. By publishing worldwide, it furthers the University's mission of dedication to excellence in teaching, scholarship, research, and clinical care.

978-1-9788-4435-3 (cloth)
978-1-9788-4434-6 (paper)
978-1-9788-4436-0 (epub)

Cataloging-in-publication data is available from the Library of Congress.
LCCN 2024047707

A British Cataloging-in-Publication record for this book is available from the British Library.

rutgersuniversitypress.org

For all students who shoulder adult responsibilities.

Contents

Insiders, Outliers

Introduction

Insiders, Outliers

During my first years on the faculty at North Carolina Central University (NCCU), I taught summer session writing classes to augment my salary. I was teaching technical writing in a windowless interior classroom during a particularly sweltering July to a group of students who were trying to get a writing intensive graduation requirement covered in five weeks. Between the heat, the pace of instruction, and the required nature of the course, showing up could have felt like a chore for all of us. But somehow it didn't. The class dynamic was positive from day one. I attributed much of this to the influence of a student whom I'll call Darius.[1] Darius was a tall, lean, exuberant social work major in his thirties whose work experience included children's recreation services. He showed up to every class offering questions, ideas, and encouragement for his classmates as they all worked on the intricacies of writing résumés and reports. By the final week, Darius had given so much energy to the class that I regarded him as nearly a co-instructor. I wanted a way to honor him and the other students who had contributed to making this demanding summer class a success. I asked the students to each nominate a classmate who was a positive influence on their learning so I could deliver a Most Valuable Peer (MVP) award on the last day. Darius was the first award winner. It was a joyous celebration to read aloud all the comments his peers wrote in their nominations.

I continued the MVP tradition during subsequent years and expanded it to all my classes. It was striking how often adult students earned these awards. Peer nomination statements about adult students reveal how valued they are in age-integrated classes. At NCCU, where one in five undergraduates are over the age of twenty-four, I could expect a handful in any given class. When I look through my archive of MVP award letters from all kinds of courses, I notice students recognizing their adult classmates for myriad qualities. Many comments reflect adults' relevant experiential knowledge: "Because of her experience with writing from her career, I think her responses on how to do things made me learn more because it has actually worked in her workplace." Nominators also frequently remark on adults' positive influence on their emotional experience of learning: "She gets me excited for class." "He gives the class excitement when he walks into the room because his eagerness to learn is always genuine." This palpable desire to learn combines with work ethic to qualify adults as "role model[s]" who are "dedicated, diligent," "involved, hardworking," and "very engaged." They are admired for their courage: "She asks the questions everyone else is afraid to." Their "helpful advice," "positive feedback," and partnership qualities on group projects are also common reasons adult students earn MVP nominations. I did not keep a copy of the award for Darius, but a nomination years later for another adult student, Stuart Parrish[2] (whom I introduce in chapter 2), synthesizes qualities of affect, knowledge, work ethic, and generosity that the two men share: "I nominate him because he has been a huge benefit to the class. He always has a positive attitude, brings laughter, wisdom, and contributive comments, and makes the class very fun and educational. He is dedicated to learning and making the most of experiences. He also works hard to help other students learn, and he is very reliable, even selflessly, unquestioningly taking up an extra burden when others experience difficulties." These MVP nominations show how important the emotional and social landscape of higher education is for students' intellectual growth. They also provide concrete reasons for the positive associations I have about working with mixed-age classrooms. Everything their younger peers appreciate about adult students is equally valuable to me as a teacher. My interest in centering them and their writing lives in my research comes out of gratitude for what they have contributed to my life as a writing teacher. However, what I understand about adult students from classroom experiences is just a starting point. *Insiders, Outliers* is the result of my desire to understand this important population as a phenomenon and as individuals. Through multiple research projects conducted with and about adult students, I learned about their highly varied educational journeys and the sources of their experiential knowledge as writers. Given how important adult students were to the culture of learning at my university, I was surprised to discover the degree to which this population has been underserved and underrepresented in key areas of higher education, including the scholarship of my field.

Adult and Nontraditional Students in U.S. Higher Education

The criteria for classifying college students as adults or nontraditional vary considerably over time, contexts, and purposes. Myriad factors including age, parenting, military service, employment, part-time enrollment, commuting, financial independence, and gaps in schooling are used inconsistently to distinguish students who differ from the full-time, straight-from-high-school, residential undergraduates who are still regarded as the traditional college population even though they are now a minority of U.S. undergraduates (NCES 2015).

Adults have been attending U.S. colleges since colonial times. Peak periods of their enrollment occurred during the early 1800s, when over a third of entering students were twenty-one years or older, and after passage of the Servicemen's Readjustment Act (the G.I. Bill) in the mid-1940s, when veterans accounted for more than a quarter of total undergraduate enrollments (Kasworm 2018). A recent study of student parents estimates, based on 2011 reports from the National Center for Educational Statistics (NCES), that 25 percent of U.S. undergraduate students are raising minor-aged children (A. F. Pearson 2019). The proportion of adult students in higher education fluctuates in relation to economic conditions, with lower adult enrollments generally tracking with periods of high employment (Blumenstyk 2018). The *Chronicle of Higher Education* reports this population as comprising 27 percent of U.S. undergraduates based on 2017 data calculations from the National Student Clearinghouse Research Center (Blumenstyk 2018). Using age parameters alone (age twenty-five and older), NCES enrollment data for 2019 indicate adult undergraduate enrollment as 25 percent of overall. When postbaccalaureate students over age twenty-five are included, the total proportion of adult postsecondary students reaches 33 percent (NCES 2021).

Using age as the sole criterion to calculate adult learners' slice of higher education offers the advantage of consistency and comparability; however, age is a blunt instrument for defining adultness. Under the related term "nontraditional" (NCES 2015; Babb 2022) and a recent variant, "post-traditional" (Soares, Gagliardi, and Nellum 2017; Blaauw-Hara 2021), adult students have been categorized within an array of students whose differences from a perceived norm are marked by specific factors that are often regarded as disadvantages in higher education (Bowl and Bathmaker 2016). For instance, NCES calculates a "risk index" that includes seven factors they mark as nontraditional: "being independent for financial aid purposes, having one or more dependents, being a single caregiver, not having a traditional high school diploma, delaying postsecondary enrollment, attending school part-time, and being employed full time" (NCES 2015). Per these more comprehensive criteria, only 26 percent of U.S. undergraduates from the 2011–2012 school year qualify as traditional.

Kasworm advocates a middle ground for adult higher education providers and researchers. Her recommendation is to rely on more than an age floor, but less than NCES's seven nontraditional factors, to establish a consistent definition of this group that prioritizes converging markers of adulthood. Her criteria include basing adult age parameters on current NCES standards; accounting for civic, work, and family responsibilities; "a gap in formal schooling"; and independence from parents that is both financial and social (2018).

While I understand Kasworm's concern about the lack of definitional consistency regarding adult and nontraditional students, customizing criteria to fit specific research aims and institutional cultures is necessary. For example, my first collaborative study of adults enrolled at a historically Black university (HBCU) was designed to learn about these students' reasons for leaving and returning to college. The investigating team understood that many of our students shoulder adult responsibilities well before the age of twenty-five. Furthermore, our students' family structures have economic and social interdependencies across generations that do not necessarily fit a white middle class template. Our recruitment materials therefore did not explicitly define age or independence parameters. Instead, we invited participants who self-identified as adult learners or nontraditional students and who had left higher education for any reason before returning for more schooling. Also, although the designations of adult and nontraditional are typically applied to undergraduate populations, I include graduate and professional degree students in my studies of adult learners because centering on the students instead of on their institutional categories prioritizes experiential life factors over academic progression. Employment experience, personal pursuits, civic engagement, and family responsibilities are more important to understanding adult students' comprehensive knowledge formation and writing lives than what level of degree they are seeking. To distinguish students with broader adult life experience from their peers whose primary responsibilities have been continuous schooling, my study of adults' writing lives does use age parameters of twenty-five and older for undergraduates and thirty and older for postbaccalaureate students. NCES data indicate that those under age thirty were a modest majority (55 percent) of postbaccalaureate students in 2019 (NCES 2021); thus, setting a floor of thirty years old enabled me to recruit a subgroup of graduate and professional degree students who were likely to have more (and more diverse) writing experiences than their younger peers.

Regardless of which parameters on adulthood are used, postsecondary enrollment data demonstrate that adult students comprise a significant proportion of the higher education landscape, and many higher education institutions seek them as a market. However, adult students continue to face obstacles to full integration into postsecondary schooling. The culture of higher education in the United States remains stubbornly premised on an imagined norm of the traditional-aged full-time student, which is no longer representative of college attendance patterns in the United States. With the exception of community colleges and other programs specifically designed for adults, postsecondary institutions do an incomplete job of creating equitable learning conditions for adult students, even when they actively recruit them. Some institutions do not make adult recruitment a priority at all. Adults' access to elite institutions is especially suppressed, and I discuss the ramifications of that in chapter 1. Inattention to this population is further reflected in the disproportionately small number of studies about them in composition research, a field that otherwise routinely centers students and their writing, including marginalized students. *Insiders, Outliers* redresses this inattention.

In contrast to discourse about adult learners that positions them as "at risk" or burdened by competing life responsibilities (NCES 2015; W. Pearson 2019; Chen, Ziskin, and Torres 2020), the cases in this book document the experiential knowledge and authority that adults derive from their personal pursuits and their roles in families, communities, and workplaces that they use to address new communicative situations, including those they encounter in higher education. Life experience is as important as schooling for informing these individuals' rhetorical and subject area knowledge and their approaches to writing. Because of the unique life trajectories of adult learners, the scope of each one's knowledge differs, thus making them an especially engaging population to work with. Ranging from their mid-twenties into their fifties, with commensurate abundance of experience, the adult students featured in this book challenge us to reimagine everything about education that has been based on younger students who attend college continuously. Although there is considerable diversity of learning within the traditional-aged undergraduate population, educators are able to make reasoned assumptions about their K–12 backgrounds and use these as a basis for action. In contrast, the lifespan learning and educational histories of adult students resist generalization. In one way or another, each adult student is an outlier, thus dramatically expanding potential areas of existing knowledge and needs that higher education personnel should take into consideration. Furthermore, adult students in higher education are more likely than their younger peers to be members of marginalized racial, ethnic, and economic groups (Bowl and Bathmaker 2016; Cohen et al. 2022). Many are thus dealing with intersectional oppressions alongside the systemic ageism they encounter in institutions shaped for younger students (Simi and Matusitz 2016).

Age bias in higher education has long been documented by scholars of adult and continuing education (Terenzini and Pascarella 1998; Sissel, Hansman, and Kasworm 2001; Donaldson and Townsend 2007; Morrow-Howell et al. 2022). Yet Collins writes that "age as a category of analysis is underemphasized within intersectionality" (2019, 196). In chapter 1, I address systemic ageism and its intersections in higher education as they pertain to persistent underservice, underrepresentation, and misrepresentation of adult students across the nation. *Insiders, Outliers* intervenes in this group's marginalization by turning toward adult students as sources of knowledge that we need in the academy. The adult undergraduate and graduate and professional degree students profiled in this book attend an HBCU that enrolls a diverse student body including those who are multiply marginalized along axes of age, race, class, gender, and/or disability. Through stories and writing samples that they draw from their personal, civic, professional, and academic lives, these students show the ethical and emotional dimensions of writing, including writing's capacity to help them resist oppression for themselves and others. The writing experiences that they interpret with me offer new ways to think about adult students as writers and rhetors, and new ways to think about how communication works across the lifespan, in and outside of academics. Their stories demonstrate the need for adult-inclusive transformations to normative educational concepts and practices.

Adult Student Research: It's Personal

My investment in adult students is grounded not only in my experiences as a professor teaching in age-integrated classrooms but also in my own experiences as a nontraditional student. When I analyze my educational background in relation to the higher education stories of the students who contributed to this book, I begin to discern how differences in age, race, class, culture, gender, family, faith, health, disability, and employment are entangled in adult college students' higher education trajectories alongside public policy, national economics, and variation in the institutional types that students attend. The marked heterogeneity of the adult student population means that each one's higher education story is layered and punctuated differently. Myriad structural and personal factors affect adults' educational decisions. Like many of the research participants whose cases inform this book, I did not attend college immediately after high school, and it took a few restarts before I had the right conditions to finish. I earned a bachelor's degree in my mid-thirties and a PhD in my forties, and I had adult responsibilities across the entirety of my postsecondary studies. During all those years, I was continuously learning, including through the periods when I was not enrolled. On-the-job and self-sponsored learning were the norms for my family and thus for me. When I was doing academics, being a worker and parent shaped many of my educational decisions, including where to apply, what shortcuts to take, and what activities to participate in outside of classes.

My past experiences as a nontraditional student exposed me to four different institutional structures where the degree to which adult students were normalized differed. I trace my postsecondary history here to show how my standpoint as a former adult student interlocks with other identities to influence the research approaches that inform this book.

My first memory of feeling a desire for college was lying on my neighbor's bedroom floor poring over her inch-thick college catalog. I was in middle school. My neighbor was eight years older and attending a private liberal arts college. I remember reading the college course descriptions about anthropology, art, biology, and creative writing and thinking they looked nothing like my middle school classes. There was so much more to learn. Despite this early interest in higher education, attending college was an anomaly in my generation of my family. Most of my five older siblings did not. Only one started college immediately after high school; I am the only one who completed a degree. We were workers, though. We all left home young and scrabbled for independence. My frugal mother said if I wanted to try college, I would qualify for more financial aid if I were independent. She had come from a poor rural farming family, and she knew how to stretch a dime. In my teens and early twenties, I shuffled through a series of short-term low-wage jobs in agriculture, construction, and retail punctuated by periods of unemployment that usually coincided with economic downturns. At the end of one recession, I landed a temporary job that led to a decade of career progression at two companies in the microscope optics industry. Thus, until my thirties, my identity as a worker was much more established than my identity as a student, even though I did sporadically enroll in credit and noncredit classes during this period.

My first brief foray into college was in my late teens. The state of Vermont had a program that granted two free community college classes to income-eligible residents. I took two art classes on this program followed by occasional noncredit continuing education courses at the same community college and studio classes at a neighborhood art school. I enjoyed them, though I assumed that any further education would be financially out of reach. However, when a recession left me unemployed in my mid-twenties, I decided I needed credentials even if it meant taking out loans. My small-town branch of the community college did not offer enough credit-bearing classes to add up to a degree. A private university admitted me to their low-residency adult degree program, which promised an expedient liberal arts degree, including ways to earn credit for prior learning. The program was completely separate from the rest of the university, and there was only one liberal studies degree offered, which depended largely on multicredit independent projects instead of classes. After just two semesters of stumbling my way through ill-defined twelve-credit projects plus racking up credit at a discount by taking as many College-Level Examination Program (CLEP) tests as I could, I decided to apply to a more traditional college where I could explore a much wider range of majors and courses. I wanted college to look more like my childhood neighbor's course catalog. But I was not quite qualified to do this yet. I had to defer my transfer to a state four-year college until I completed a noncredit remedial math class at the community college. Meanwhile, I started a job in the optics industry. When the temporary position turned permanent, I put an indefinite pause on my studies.

At the age of twenty-seven, I became unemployed again. The company I had worked for supplied optical filters for researchers studying the universe, and green fluorescent protein, and the human genome, all of which seemed way more interesting than the job I had held there of assembling and quality-checking instrument optics. I wanted to be *using* microscopes, not making parts for them. I knew that shifting from being an unemployed optical technician to starting a career in the sciences would require much more education. I enrolled full-time at the regional public college with the intention of becoming a biology major. However, I withdrew after one semester when my responsibilities at a new job expanded dramatically. This was another technical position but at a new optical company. I went from unemployed to working part-time to overtime all the time at an employee-owned start-up company where advancement was likely if the business succeeded. The pace was exciting, and the financial stakes seemed high. There just was no time for school.

Seven years later at the age of thirty-four, I had a family and I was making good money. I enjoyed learning the many roles necessary at this growing company. I did technical writing, created manufacturing protocols, ran the quality assurance program, and was responsible for hiring, training, and coordinating workflows in two departments. I had risen to a quasi-management position on the basis of skills acquired on the job, not academic credentials. Yet I still dreamed of doing something other than manufacturing. Leary of debt, I realized I could finally afford to explore other options if I sold my shares back to the company. Returning part-time to the state college was my way to test the waters. This time it felt right. I left my job to enroll full-time without declaring a major, anticipating I would figure out a new profession along the way to a degree.

Starting all over again learning side by side with classmates who were fifteen years younger than me was humbling. I felt disconcerted by losing the professional authority I had earned from scratch as a senior technician in a multimillion-dollar enterprise. "Nontraditional" was a prevalent term in the 1990s to describe adult students and others who differed from full-time undergraduates still dependent on their families (Horn and Caroll 1996). I identified as nontraditional because it suggested the matrix of differences that separated me from my peers. My professional experience was only one factor. I was also older and queerer than my classmates. I was supporting a family. I had a choppy educational background. At the community college and the adult degree program, older students were the norm. It was different at the regional state college. There I was one of maybe two adults in each of my classes, older than some of my professors. My young classmates seemed to regard college as a given, as compulsory as K–12 had been. For me, it was not. Every semester required a new cost-benefit analysis. Every course was a deliberate choice.

This potentially alienating situation was mitigated by finally having the course variety I craved. My advisor explained that I could ask professors to waive prerequisites so I could enroll in the advanced classes that attracted me. I felt the patchiness of my past education, but it was socially and intellectually satisfying to bond with another student parent, to collaborate in mixed-age teams on creative projects, and to meet faculty who treated me as an experienced learner even though I was new to the material at hand and lacked a common vocabulary about academic writing. (I wrote well enough to test out of first-year composition, but when a professor encouraged students to go beyond the five-paragraph essay formula, I had no idea what formula she was talking about.) The professional and technical writing I had done on the job did not resemble the academic writing I was assigned, but the professors at the state college provided feedback that I could learn from. They also encouraged me to keep expressing my ideas, no matter how strange they seemed or how hard it was for me to move from noticing and describing to making well-structured claims. They welcomed my attempts to integrate what I knew from my adult life with the new meanings in their courses. In a Shakespeare class, for instance, I made connections between dramatized royal power struggles and interpersonal workplace drama I had experienced at the optics company. For a sociology class, I observed the gendered dynamics at my kids' school playground. In this way, I gradually found my footing as an adult student.

I now understand that I experienced an unusual degree of adult-inclusive pedagogy and mentoring that extended beyond standard coursework. After taking one contemporary rhetoric course, I wanted to explore more beyond my final paper, so a sociology professor and an English professor co-mentored me in an interdisciplinary independent study about the rhetoric of poverty. They urged me to present at an undergraduate research conference. Another English professor asked me to guest lecture in their children's literature class based on a paper I had written about the rhetoric of book covers for queer young adult fiction. These professors also suggested graduate school; the advanced experiences with writing, research, and presenting that they had invited me to try made the idea feasible. My professors' encouragement was matched by my extended family's support, which helped me remain continuously enrolled for five undergraduate semesters until I completed an English degree at the age of thirty-six. That was nineteen years and three kids after graduating high school. I was accepted into a doctoral program soon after. Completing the PhD required a fraction of the time I had taken to earn a BA.

My educational backstory helps me see the adult students I teach and study. The nontraditional identities of such students may go unrecognized, or students may opt to pass as traditional aged in contexts where they are a minority (A. F. Pearson 2019). Yet when I introduce myself on the first day of a class and mention I earned my bachelor's degree in my thirties, I see who nods and makes eye contact. Being out about my nontraditional identity opens potential lines of communication with students who may feel like outliers themselves. Our experiences are not the same, with racial difference being a decisive difference, yet some aspects of my undergraduate history consistently resonate with adult students at North Carolina Central University. Priorities regarding finances and family form our most common connections. I personally understand the dance between work, school, and caregiving that many students at NCCU must perform, whether they are over the age of twenty-four or not. I also recognize that students' family members play complex roles in their educational decisions. It is well established, for instance, that parental educational background has a dominant influence on higher education attainment that holds true for students who attend college later in life (Cohen et al. 2022). Although my father's influence was somewhat muted by my siblings' ambivalence toward formal education, his master's degree nevertheless made my odds of attaining a bachelor's degree higher than the odds for first-generation students.

The stories I hear from adult learners in my classes and research suggest that a broader concept of family, particularly among non-white students, could account for some of the patterns of adult enrollment and degree attainment that may not be evident from national datasets that mark parental education but look no further into the influence of extended family (NCES 2022b). The category of "first generation," for example, is important for tracking socioeconomic differences in postsecondary outcomes, but it is based on a skimpy definition of family (Cataldi, Bennet, and Chen 2018). In contrast to this nuclear model, family for many students at NCCU is a more generous concept. They mention being inspired to return to school when they see their grandparents, spouses, cousins, children, and grandchildren—biologically related and otherwise—engaged in academics. Black feminist theorists demonstrate that family networks extend beyond the parent-child relationships that are documented in white-normative educational research, and indeed beyond biological kin (Collins 2000; hooks 2000). Although I am white, nonbiological kinship nevertheless influenced my educational aspirations. Partnering in my early thirties into an extended family that had a nearly universal pattern of advanced degree attainment over multiple generations factored into what I came to see as desirable and possible for myself. Graduate school had been unimaginable during my first tentative enrollments in college. However, my partner's mother had earned her doctorate as a single parent, and that fact changed my perspective. Thus, in addition to white racial privilege, the financial buffer from my prior career, and the inclusive practices of my professors at the state college, the cumulative advantages that underwrote my eventual attainment of three postsecondary degrees included the encouragement and model provided by this extended nonbiological family. I was finally in a position to extend some of this advantage to others once I began my academic career.

Adult Students and Adult Learner Research at North Carolina Central University

NCCU is the smallest of the three public universities in the Triangle region of North Carolina comprised of the Durham, Chapel Hill, and Raleigh metro areas. NCCU enrolls about 8,000 students, more than three-quarters of whom are undergraduates. Comparing 2021 enrollment demographics to those of neighboring UNC-Chapel Hill and NC State University, NCCU educates higher proportions of undergraduates who are minorities (91 percent), women (70 percent), transfer students (8 percent), part-time students (19 percent), Pell Grant recipients (57 percent), and those age twenty-five and older (18 percent) (IPEDS n.d.). On a morning in 2009 when I was on campus to interview for a position there, I encountered a woman dressed in scrubs sitting on a hallway floor outside a classroom. "You look tired," I said. She told me she had come straight to campus from her overnight shift at a hospital to get to her morning class, and she was just taking a break before the next. This was my first indication of the complex lives of NCCU's adult students, who, eight years later, would become the center of my research agenda.

The adult students I worked with during twelve years on the faculty at NCCU were remarkably diverse in their educational backgrounds, writing experiences, and ages. Although one in five undergraduates at NCCU was over twenty-four years of age, they were not highly visible in the first-year writing program that I directed. My most frequent connections with adult learners occurred in sophomore through graduate level courses in which young parents, grandparents, veterans, and other adults made a strong impression in age-integrated classrooms. What I noticed about their classroom interactions and their writing sparked my interest in learning more about their lives and writing experiences.

During my research for this book, I did not formally investigate faculty and staff attitudes about adult students, but I noticed that my colleagues regarded teaching mixed age groups as the norm. We understood that many students juggled jobs and/or family caregiving responsibilities with their studies. Some university services were well oriented toward adults. Students reported that staff at Transfer Services, Veterans Affairs, and NCCU Online understood adult needs. Several academic units offered degree options tailored for adults. For instance, a BS in behavioral and social sciences was approved in 2015 to attract returning adult undergraduates as NCCU's first designated completer degree. Adult-oriented postbaccalaureate offerings included the law school's part-time evening program, the library science program's fully online master's option, and a master's in public administration that could be earned via an executive track designed for experienced professionals. However, focus groups and interviews with adult students revealed that such adult-inclusivity occurred in pockets rather than being broadly reflected in the institutional culture. They pointed to offices that closed at 5:00 P.M. and orientation events geared only to younger people as signals that adult students were not a priority. The university's preoccupation with traditional-aged students was furthermore evident in inflexible administrative rhetoric about retention and degree completion. For example, NCCU Chancellor Saunders-White's top priority at the start of her tenure and repeated frequently to both internal and external audiences was expedient degree attainment. In an inaugural press release, she announced her primary goal, "We need to ensure that our students are crossing the stage in four years" (quoted in Hernandez 2013). Although external factors including educational funding metrics exert conformist ideological pressures that are difficult for university administrators to buck, the chancellor's goal ignores at least one-fifth of the student population who would benefit from normalizing variation in educational pace. Faculty routinely practice differentiated instruction in recognition of variability in students' interests and needs; institutions could likewise adopt differentiated retention and graduation models that reflect the truths about the students they serve.

At the highest levels in the University of North Carolina System, ubiquitous neoliberal rhetorics of efficiency regarding degree progression coexisted uneasily with desires to attract and serve the adult student market. For instance, the statewide 2017–2022 strategic plan declared "we must expand the pipelines to nontraditional students and adult learners" (UNCGA 2017, 10) while simultaneously banging the drum for "on-time graduation" in four years (5), two goals that are at odds. In April 2017, the University of North Carolina System convened to discuss recruitment and degree completion rates for adult learners at all state institutions. This two-day gathering reflected enhanced system-wide attention to the estimated 1.1 million state residents who were designated as having some college but no degree (UNC 2017). Speakers emphasized a familiar quartet of performance metrics: enrollment, retention, persistence, and graduate rates, as these pertained to adult students. I discuss implications of these designations in chapter 1 because of their normative functions that render this population as either a market, an anomaly, or a problem rather than regarding adult students as constituents of higher education who contribute to reshaping our institutions.

Shortly after the state's Adult Learners Convening, NCCU issued an internal request for proposals to fund multidisciplinary projects that addressed some area of need relevant to the university's strategic plan. My colleague Stefanie Frigo, who coordinates the interdisciplinary studies major, was the only faculty member serving on a university committee focused on adult learners.

She was well aware of nontraditional students' needs for flexibility in degree pathways. She and I approached the call for proposals as an opportunity to design a research project that could address the university's contradictory rhetoric about adult students and degree progression. Our study of students' reasons for leaving and returning to higher education was the first of several participatory adult student research projects that inform this book's findings.

I discuss the objectives and approaches of this adult-centered research agenda more in chapter 2. Chapters 3 through 5 illustrate the results of such a research agenda by disclosing new understandings about adult students and their writing. The collective findings from these projects indicate that the complex personal, educational, workforce, and writing histories of adult students defy reduction. Their job histories are particularly complex, including many students reporting three or more significant employment sector changes over their lives. Layered onto this are myriad family responsibilities and forms of community engagement, showing that adults are involved in an abundance of nonacademic activities that both develop and require knowledge and rhetorical sophistication. This prior (and concurrent) learning is all over the map, making adult students an especially engaging, norm-defying population to work with who have unique capacities to contribute to classrooms, research, and institutional change projects. In *Insiders, Outliers*, I make these capacities visible; understanding this diverse group as a significant asset to U.S. higher education empowers rethinking the academic enterprise from its conceptual frameworks through its fundamental activities of teaching, student services, and research.

The Goals of This Book

My aim with this book is to face the underrepresentation of adult students in the field of writing studies and to do something about it. I show how this discipline-specific inattention is a manifestation of the broader marginalization of adult students in higher education. I also analyze the limitations of normative educational concepts in light of adult students' diverse experiential knowledge. While it is important to theorize about academia and marginalized populations, which I do, it is equally important to show why it is desirable to remake writing across the disciplines into an age-inclusive endeavor. That requires comprehending adults' life breadth of intellectual activities and the values that infuse their academic pursuits.

I intend for the book's focus on the writing lives of adult undergraduate, graduate, and professional degree students to help readers reimagine writing across the lifespan as an ethical and emotional practice, thus changing ways we teach it in and across the disciplines. My most ambitious goal with this book, however, is to contribute to the development of institutional cultures that are responsive to the entire age spectrum of students. Being a student is an affective and intellectual social experience that individuals engage in across many stages of life. Every corner of our institutions should reflect that. To reap the societal and institutional benefits of centering this population, they need to be recognized not just in pockets and stratified parts of postsecondary education but throughout higher education systems and institutions. My desire is thus for readers to leverage the ideas in this book to transform policies, services, programs, curricula, extracurriculars, research agendas, and classes since these are material differences that can flow from changing the ways we think about higher education and the students it serves.

The Structure of This Book

Insiders, Outliers is organized to illuminate the value of research about this population with specific attention to their educational histories and lifewide writing experiences. I establish the grounds for my argument by showing that adult students are currently underrepresented in scholarship about writing, a phenomenon with roots in higher education's structural ageism. To redress these inequities, I propose a rhizomatic philosophy of adult-centered educational research illustrated with methodological stories from the participatory research that informs this book. I then develop cases that focus on adult students as writers to offer conceptual possibilities that resist the normative frameworks in higher education that render this population as outliers rather than integral members. The case-based chapters are organized to advance understandings of writers' ethical and emotional agency as enacted across a breadth of life activities. These include students' activism to make educational institutions live up to their liberatory potential, or at least their stated equity and inclusion principles.

Chapter 1 examines the relationship between the institutional stratification of adult students and their resulting underrepresentation in writing studies scholarship. These are quantifiable interconnected manifestations of structural ageism in higher education that contextualize my qualitative project of countering adult students' marginalization as writers. My analysis of age stratification focuses on enrollment patterns in the Triangle region of North Carolina, where the students in this book live, work, and attend school. I trace the compounding effects of racism, classism, and ageism that result in the extreme stratification of students across open-access, selective, and midrange institutions, noting its effects on age bias in educational scholarship, including focused analysis on the underrepresentation of adult students in rhetoric and composition scholarship. From this evidence, I propose an anti-ageist intersectional research agenda that centers adult students.

Chapter 2 is a methodological narrative about my attempts to instantiate the anti-ageist research agenda that I advocate. I tell a series of fieldwork stories from my work with student participants and research partners as I learned ways to pay attention to their unusual experiences with education and writing. The chapter argues for adaptation of Deleuze and Guattari's rhizomatic theory, which has informed other researchers' methodologies for studying the heterogeneous adult student population. Its capaciousness reflects my development of situationally specific methods to account for unruly, multidirectional, outlier aspects of the educational histories and writing lives of adult students. Methods include participant-centered, feminist co-interpretive interviewing practices that regard participants as experts on their own lives who have capacity to lead researchers to new meanings. Stories from the field show how rhizomatic and collaborative research practices work when adult students bring different standpoints, expertise, and interests to the enterprise.

Chapter 3 is the first of three case-based chapters that illuminate areas of prior knowledge in adult students' writing lives to yield concepts applicable to adult-inclusive higher education. This chapter is the only one developed from a single case. Tamara Vanie is a married Black mother of five whose circuitous educational journey to an associate's degree took sixteen years across four states and five institutions. She is also a veteran, dancer, social entrepreneur, and educational activist who uses self-sponsored writing across many of her life activities. Her educational history and selected writing experiences from her personal and public life call into question the usage of the term "persistence" in higher education discourse. I pose a more expansive concept of "persisting" to center adult learners rather than higher education systems in analysis of adult students' educational and life trajectories and their literate activities. In both her personal and public life, writing functions as a means for addressing problems, including racism and sexism. I use Black feminist theory and borrow Tamara's term, "creating movement," to consider situations when Tamara writes as a means to persist (move through and toward) or resist (move against) in these situations. Tamara's scenarios furthermore suggest possibilities for resisting normative academic preoccupations about writing as an end in itself, instead showing it to be a vital means for putting principled action into motion.

In chapter 4, I consider the limitations of the college-to-career paradigm in higher education given the significant workforce knowledge that many adult students accrue prior to and concurrent with their educations. With positions that range from early career clerical, call center, and nursing assistant jobs to senior roles as the vice president of a bank and the compliance officer for a medical system, fifteen students ages thirty to mid-fifties provide insider knowledge about the ethical dimensions of writing on the job. Many reveal a depth of thinking that is at odds with higher education's positioning of students—even graduate and professional degree students—as career novices. In examples of their writing of handbooks for several fields, ethical deliberation emerges as a common theme in the work lives of these students. To develop a concept of ethical agency more fully, I discuss workplace writers' negotiations of ethically complex situations in two sectors: health care and higher education. I show how these writers and their writing are treated at their workplaces; the consequences of their professional writing; and how these workplace authors negotiate control over the style, content, and purposes of their writing in situations of unequal power. Adult students' retention of their own ethical stances and authorial voices even under the constraints of workplaces holds promise for helping students across ages and disciplines discern possibilities for writing with ethical agency in their professional lives.

Chapter 5 theorizes emotion's relationship to writing through analysis of emotionally saturated situations in adult undergraduates' personal and academic lives, focusing on writing that is self-initiated rather than that which is assigned. I combine cross-disciplinary theories of emotional agency with theories of writing to discuss the ways that adult students use writing as a mode of feeling, recognize emotion as a signal of rhetorical exigence, and put both emotion and writing into circulation to effect changes in themselves and the people and institutions that matter to them. Analysis of brief scenarios of writing with emotion in the personal lives of undergraduates Paula Thacker, Lisa Fakir, and Gary Lassiter are followed by two detailed cases situated in academia that are provided by undergraduate coinvestigator Adrienne Long. A psychology major who founded the adult student organization at NCCU, Adrienne draws on family and professional knowledge to deploy critical emotional agency in her correspondence with university administrators, modeling for them how to address the needs and interests of adult students like herself. In the process, she articulates the dual identities of undergraduate and adult that jointly inform her rhetorical stances and push at the boundaries of normative constructions of college students. Co-interpretive analysis of Adrienne's and other participants' writing scenarios furthermore repairs conceptual schisms between intellect and emotion by demonstrating that emotion fuels the rhetorical action through which writers change themselves and their contexts.

The conclusion synthesizes lessons from the cases of the writers in this book, who are eager to learn and be respected for their knowledge and are insightfully critical of structures and practices in higher education that exclude them. I argue that adult students are uniquely valuable members of our postsecondary institutions who contribute to collective efforts to rewrite the cultures of higher education with equity and justice as guiding principles.

I have found it challenging to accept that aspects of higher education that I am intimately involved in perpetuate the ageism that permeates academia. That this is largely through inattention rather than intent does not mitigate the need for changes. Through the insights of the many adult students who have shared their experiences, this book offers criticism and its more hopeful bedfellow. It suggests creative possibilities for transforming higher education with adult students so that it works for all students.

1

Confronting Ageism in Higher Education

Most of this book centers on analysis of adult students' writing and rhetorical experiences that they have accrued across their professional and personal lives. This multifaceted experiential knowledge is important to understand because it is part of what distinguishes the large population of adult learners from their younger classmates. Neither the knowledge domains of adulthood nor the full population of adult postsecondary students have received enough attention yet in scholarship about degree-seeking students. To demonstrate this and to understand why it is so, I take a wide lens in this chapter by examining the relationship between two major contexts for my research. These are institutional stratification of adult students and their severe underrepresentation in scholarship about students, particularly in writing studies. These phenomena are interconnected manifestations of structural ageism in higher education.

Ageism operates on a systemic scale that is evident from the macro level of federal policies through the micro level of one-to-one interactions. In adult students' everyday academic lives, ageism bleeds into interactions with university personnel and peers as well as into pedagogies, curricular design, campus communications, and institutional policies that disregard this population. However, my aim in chapter 1 is to present ageism as it is structured into the larger formations of higher education. Quantifying this group's absences and presences across institutions and scholarship contextualizes my qualitative project of countering adult students' marginalization as writers.

Ageism and Its Intersections in Higher Education

Given that one-quarter of U.S. undergraduates are aged twenty-five or older, it may seem paradoxical to argue that this large population is harmed by age bias. Adults enroll in significant numbers, and the most tuition-dependent strata of institutions generally regard them as a desirable market. Yet the real dimensions of college student age are frequently overlooked in the academy. This has direct consequences for adult students' long-term prospects and day-to-day experiences of higher education.

People in their mid-twenties through thirties—the majority of adult students—are not generally regarded as being subject to ageism in the wider culture. This is because our understanding of ageism in the United States is largely shaped by labor laws intended to prevent discrimination against older workers; the protection afforded by the Age Discrimination in Employment Act of 1967 does not apply to workers younger than age forty (U.S. Equal Employment Opportunity Commission n.d.). Scholarship on ageism in higher education is far more often about the academic workforce than about students (Bunch and Palladi 2017; Hendrix 2021; Johnson 2021). Yet the World Health Organization (WHO) notes that ageism is not tethered to worksites nor to a specific age threshold but instead is identified with cultural role expectations (*Global Report on Ageism* 2021), including the role of student. This body's discussion of institutional ageism across nations and sectors calls out the United States as a location in which ageism is "facilitated by the historically age-segregated structure of higher education" and is evident in both structural and attitudinal impingement upon adult students' postsecondary studies (2021, 30). One far-reaching effect of ageism in higher education is the inability to perceive adult students as significant because the cultural expectation of college student identity is so firmly normalized as young adult. They are no longer a majority (NCES 2015), yet students in their late teens who enroll full-time directly from high school with parental support are represented as the norm in popular media from *Animal House* to *Pitch Perfect, A Different World* to *Grown-ish*. Decade after decade, fictionalizations of college life reinscribe higher education's persistent youth-centrism despite enrollment patterns to the contrary. Overrepresentation of youth in scholarship about postsecondary students has a similar effect.

Like racism and other forms of oppression, ageism and its intersections are of sweeping consequence yet so ubiquitous as to go unnoticed except by those who endure them. Ageism in the academy affects every aspect of adult students' higher education experiences from their recruitment and lack thereof to the debt they carry when they leave institutions, with or without a degree. It prevents adult college students from benefiting from the full array of educational opportunities because they are frequently disregarded in university policies, objectives, and practices (Simi and Matusitz 2016). Scholars who promote the nascent Age Friendly University movement argue that age "should be integrated into any evaluation of inclusivity in higher education" (Silverstein et al. 2022, e49). Yet diversity, equity, and inclusion efforts on behalf of students frequently neglect to address ageism. Age also remains rarely integrated into intersectional analysis (Collins 2019). Adult-centered and age-inclusive research are unusual even among researchers who investigate a matrix of race, gender, class, and other identities to address inequality in higher education (Byrd, Brunn-Bevel, and Ovink 2019; Mitchell, Simmons, and Greyerbiehl 2014). The exceptions point to the contextual dimensions of age norming and the value of including age or other measures of adulthood in analytical matrices. For instance, an intersectional theorist notes that for women veteran college students, "age had faint magnitude in the military, but it gained in apparent magnitude on campus when surrounded by younger peers" (Iverson 2014, 144). Another age-inclusive analysis is a report from the Institute for Women's Policy Research about Black single mothers in college that identifies structural obstacles faced by this subset of adult students (Turner and White 2023). The report's attention to gender, race, and class in relation to student parents' educational outcomes is designed to inform student advocates and policymakers about which measures are likely to have the greatest impact on educational equity for this multiply marginalized population. These kinds of investigations contribute to understandings about how ageism is amplified by intersections with racism and classism to result in this population's unequal educational opportunities. Analysis of adult enrollment makes this inequality tangible.

Age Stratification in Institutional Enrollment

My analysis of enrollment patterns in the region of North Carolina where I conducted the research for this book shows the effects of structural ageism in the extreme age stratification of students across different institutional types. For example, adult students are largely absent from elite institutions while being overrepresented at tuition-dependent broad-access institutions that tend to be financially vulnerable, much like the students they serve. Racism and classism compound the effects of ageism in these stratification findings. These enrollment patterns have sweeping ramifications that include the extent to which adult students are illegible to researchers.

In the introduction to this book, I discuss in broad strokes the national enrollment data about adult students. Analyses by scholars of higher education stratification do not consistently attend to student age, but they do show that low-income and minoritized students remain persistently underrepresented in the elite and super elite strata of U.S. higher education (Taylor and Cantwell 2019), while they are overrepresented in broad-access institutions (Crisp et al.

2019). Adult enrollment patterns closely parallel institutional stratification of low-income and racial and ethnic minority students. The added dimension of age bias compounds the marginalization of adult students who are also members of these other minoritized groups. In this chapter, I tighten the scope of enrollment analysis to the region in which I conducted studies of adult learners. This places these patterns into a local context relevant to the cases presented in subsequent chapters.

The Triangle, or Research Triangle, of North Carolina is defined by three municipalities: Raleigh, Durham, and Chapel Hill, and the major research universities therein. In addition to North Carolina State University, UNC-Chapel Hill, and Duke University, other postsecondary educational institutions in the region represent a spectrum of types that include the public HBCU where I was employed, public and private not-for-profit two-year and four-year colleges (including two private HBCUs and a women's college), and several for-profit institutions. Within this concentrated region, it is possible to discern the enrollment stratification that is both a symptom of and a factor in the perpetuation of systemic ageism in higher education. I argue that this stratification plays an outsized role in the underrepresentation of the adult student population as a subject of research. Age bias that results in institutional stratification is a more significant factor in the persistent underrepresentation of this population than any attributes of adult students themselves.

Pairing information from the Carnegie Classification of Institutions of Higher Education (2023) and National Center for Education Statistics (NCES 2021, 2022a), I compare adult enrollments across seven of the colleges and universities in the region, selected to represent diverse institutional types. Close attention to their enrollment data helps tell the stories behind adults' underrepresentation and underservice. The first story is about their stratification into some kinds of institutions and away from others. I focus on undergraduate enrollment rather than total enrollment in this cross-institutional analysis. I examine fall 2019, the semester I began conducting interviews for the Writing Lives study at NCCU. In addition to comparing enrollments by age, I also document enrollments of Black students in the region to indicate what a limited intersectional analysis reveals about age, race, and educational opportunity as these pertain to adult student representation in research. Although there are many different racial and ethnic groups among adult students, Black students are most relevant to this analysis due to their prevalence in the southeast region of the U.S. and at my research site. The U.S. 2020 Census indicates that 12.1 percent of the U.S. population and 20.2 percent of the North Carolina population is Black or African American (Shrider et al. 2021). At 13 percent, the total enrollment rate of Black undergraduates in the United States is slightly higher than the proportion of Black people in the United States, suggesting that a 20 percent rate of Black college enrollment would be

Table 1.1
Fall 2019 adult and Black undergraduate enrollments in seven North Carolina institutions

Institutions	Research activity	Total undergrad *n*	25+ undergrad *n*	25+ undergrad %	Black undergrad *n*	Black undergrad %
Total U.S.		16,557,539	4,195,822	25.4	2,100,200	13
More selective						
Duke	very high	6,649	25	0.38	583	8.77
UNC-CH	very high	19,154	541	2.82	1,548	8.08
NCSU	very high	25,973	1,726	6.65	1,515	5.83
Inclusive						
Meredith		1,528	73	4.78	131	8.57
NCCU		6,101	1,108	18.16	4,771	78.20
Open-access[a]						
DTCC		4,949	2,143	43.30	1,602	32.37
Strayer-NC		5,333	4,549	85.30	4,085	76.60

SOURCES: Enrollment data: Integrated Postsecondary Education Data System, National Center for Education Statistics (IPEDS n.d.) Institutional selectivity and research activity: Carnegie Classification of Institutions of Higher Education (2023).

[a] Carnegie broadly classifies these among inclusive institutions. In practice, they are both open-access to students who have high school diplomas or equivalent.

logical to extrapolate for North Carolina. The institutional differences in regional undergraduate enrollment of both Black students and students over the age of twenty-four—which are not mutually exclusive categories—help tell the story about compounding factors in adult students' marginalization. The three institutions that serve the highest proportion of adult undergraduates also serve the highest proportion of Black undergraduates. NCES data is limited in that it is not possible to determine what rates of Black adult undergraduates are enrolled in the United States nor at specific institutions, but the similarly stratified measures of these two populations within Triangle region institutions indicate the presence of intersectional forces that track multiply marginalized students into inclusive and open-access institutions while suppressing their access to elite education.

Over-Represented in Open-Access Institutions

Two-thirds of the over 10,000 adult undergraduates represented in this regional comparison attend two small open-access institutions: a community college and the local branch of a for-profit university. These institutions also enroll an outsized 40 percent of the Black students in the dataset and have by far the highest rates of part-time students in the group. Data on Pell eligibility—a proxy for reporting low income—is unavailable for the for-profit university because only 5 percent of its students attend full-time. Of the 20 percent of students at the community college who attend full-time, half are Pell eligible (IPEDS n.d.). In terms of age, race, and class, marginalized students in the Triangle region of North Carolina are likely to attend one of these open-access institutions, where the costs of access diverge markedly depending on institutional type.

Durham Technical Community College is one of fifty-nine community colleges in the state system and one of two in the Triangle. Adult students are a traditional population at Durham Tech; prior to 2015 they comprised a majority of students; by 2019 that proportion decreased to 43 percent (IPEDS n.d.), a decline that is consistent with national community college enrollment trends (Berg et al. 2023). A third of Durham Tech students are Black. The institution offers free basic education and high school equivalency courses. It also provides relatively low-cost career credentials, continuing education, and associate's degrees with baccalaureate transfer options. Analysis of the national college enrollment patterns of Black single mothers shows that two-thirds of Black women in higher education attend community college at some point in their studies (Turner and White 2023), thus indicating interplay between age, race, and enrollment stratification.

Strayer University is a national chain marketing in the mid-Atlantic, south, and south-central United States, which attracted the second-highest enrollments in online universities among North Carolina residents in 2019 (Smalley 2021). Although the parent company is large, the Strayer-NC branch is classified as a small private for-profit master's university with predominantly online degree programs (Carnegie 2023). The undergraduate majority is adult, Black, and part-time students who seek four-year degrees. The adult enrollment is 85 percent, almost double the rate of the community college, and by far the largest enrollment rate of students over the age of twenty-four among the seven selected institutions. Their enrollment accounts for 45 percent of adults across the institutional comparison dataset. It also nearly matches the HBCU in Black student enrollment. This overrepresentation of adult and Black students occurs despite Strayer-NC's startlingly high tuition. In 2023, Strayer charged $508 per credit hour versus $76 for in-state residents at Durham Tech, according to their respective websites. Strayer-NC furthermore exceeds in-state tuition at UNC-Chapel Hill, the state's flagship, by over $200 per credit hour.[1] Although the enrollment numbers at Strayer-NC suggest inclusive accessibility for marginalized populations of adult and Black students, the debt outcomes combined with low graduation rates and poor value of credentials have yielded criticism that for-profit chains like Strayer practice predatory inclusion of such groups (Smith et al. 2023). McMillan Cottom writes that "for-profit colleges are distinct from not-for-profit colleges in that their long-term viability depends upon acute, sustained, socioeconomic inequalities. All of higher education benefits from inequality in some way, but online for-profit colleges exclusively, by definition, rely on persistent inequalities as a business model" (2017, 21). Adult students at for-profits pay dearly for accessibility that does not correlate to opportunity. And yet, their marginalization at most four-year universities in the region suggests that educational options for this group are severely constrained (Taylor and Cantwell 2019).

Excluded from Selective Universities

In contrast to the open-access institutions in the area, the three research universities that define the contours of the Research Triangle are bluntly categorized as "more selective," and that selectivity disproportionately excludes adult students. Carnegie defines the two factors of selectivity as admission rates and scores on standardized SAT or ACT tests. Under Taylor and Cantwell's (2019) more nuanced classification system, Duke exists among "super elite" private universities in that its secure financial position combined with extraordinarily high demand enable it to enact the most selective admissions practices, practices that are neither sustainable nor desirable for publicly funded universities and that function to exclude adult undergraduates almost categorically. The rate of adult undergraduate enrollment is so small at Duke that the twenty-five undergraduates over the age of twenty-four that attended in 2019 did not even approach one-half of one percent of the overall undergraduate population; it also enrolls the lowest rate of Pell-eligible students among institutions in the region. Furthermore, Duke's Black student enrollments are four points below the national average. Opportunities for degree-seeking adult undergraduates at Duke to develop any sense of shared identity thus seem unlikely, as does the potential for research faculty to perceive them as an identifiable population of interest.

The exceedingly low number of adults enrolled as undergraduates at Duke is barely improved upon at the state's flagship, UNC-Chapel Hill; at under 3 percent their presence is still extremely small given the public mission of the university. Among the three more selective institutions in the comparison group, only North Carolina State University (NCSU), a land grant public university, admits adult students at a rate that would make their presence somewhat palpable to research faculty and each other. There, an average of two adults would be evident in a class of thirty undergraduates. That proportion is about what I experienced in the small public regional college where I earned a bachelor's degree in my mid-thirties. That was just enough adults to recognize that we shared a nontraditional identity, and just enough for faculty and staff to have some awareness of us as a population of interest. Per Carnegie, NCSU also differs from Duke and UNC-Chapel Hill in that it has a higher proportion of undergraduates to graduate students, and it educates slightly more nonresidential, transfer, and part-time students.[2] The university demonstrates consciousness of adult students in its research mission by employing research faculty who specialize in adult learning. Several master's degrees in adult and community college education are offered through the College of Education, which further distinguish NCSU from its R1 neighbors in terms of visible regard for adult students as a population worthy of inquiry. Nevertheless, the higher rate of adults enrolled at NCSU, shy of 7 percent, remains little over one-quarter of the national average, and the proportion of Black students is the lowest of all seven institutions in this regional comparison.

A Market in the Middle

On a national scale, the large number of institutions that exist between the poles of open access and highly selective, and between negligible and high research activity, differ across multiple characteristics including in their adult student populations. Broad-access private colleges and universities often regard adult students as a desirable market, especially as they seek to manage diminishing traditional age enrollments, a trend referred to as the demographic cliff (Grawe 2018). In the Triangle region, several small private institutions and the public regional HBCU where I worked occupy this middle ground. These institutions' efforts to attract and retain adult students may be more evident on their websites than in their enrollment numbers. For example, Meredith College is a small private women's college at which the rate of adult students is currently just under 5 percent, and Black students enroll at a rate similar to the most selective universities in the area. Yet beyond the enrollment data, there is evidence of outreach to adult and Black learners on Meredith's website. Whereas the websites of the two least adult-inclusive institutions in the Triangle, Duke and UNC-Chapel Hill, relegate adult marketing to their nondegree continuing education programs, Meredith announces an array of services specifically for degree-seeking adult students and recognizes multiple entry points and goals for this population. The images and profiles they use represent students of diverse races and ethnicities.[3] This attention to adult students as a heterogeneous group suggests that administrators have some awareness of the sizeable potential market comprised of adults, even if this group is not currently a significant proportion of the college's enrollments.

Also between the extremes of Duke and Strayer lies NCCU, an institution that achieves closest to the national average for adult enrollments (18 percent), and the highest percentage of Black students (78 percent) and Pell-eligible students (72 percent) among the seven comparison institutions. As I have noted in this book's introduction, NCCU markets their online offerings and several undergraduate, certificate, professional, and graduate programs specifically to adult students; their public relations department routinely circulates stories about adult students' achievements. Such students at institutions like Meredith and NCCU furthermore have the potential to be regarded as a population of interest not just for institutional solvency but also for research. This is because these kinds of institutions do have research missions alongside their teaching emphasis. Carnegie's classification system misses any of this activity because it fails to differentiate the research outputs of institutions with fewer than twenty doctoral programs, effectively representing the Strayers and the NCCUs as equivalent in this regard. Yet research expectations and infrastructures below Carnegie's threshold vary considerably in ways that affect whether adult students have opportunities to be represented in research activity. For example, consistent with many regional universities, NCCU faculty have high teaching and service responsibilities and are not expected to publish at the rate of their peers at research institutions, although the expectation of some research activity remains. The institutional support for conducting research is commensurately lesser, with financial constraints on research activity compounded by a century of discriminatory underfunding that remains typical of public HBCUs in the UNC System (Arnette 2015; Boland and Gasman 2014; Taylor et al. 2020). Yet as a regional public four-year university, NCCU's research culture is much greater than at public community colleges and private for-profits in the Triangle, where research is not a part of the institutional missions.

The Effect of Age Stratification on Research

The stratified adult undergraduate enrollment across these seven Triangle-area universities and colleges suggests that structural ageism functions in recruitment and admissions processes in proportion to institutional prestige. Diverse adult students enroll across the spectrum of institutional types, but their proportions are stratified such that they are a more significant presence at teaching-mission institutions that have lower barriers to student access, higher reliance on contingent faculty, and less research infrastructure than selective institutions (NCES 2023). I do not claim that all prospective adult students are logical candidates for highly selective institutions. But there is no justifying a mere 3 percent or 0.5 percent adult enrollment rate on the basis of merit. These rates furthermore skew research about undergraduates such that the traditional-aged population is overrepresented in scholarship because they are overrepresented in elite universities. Faculty at selective research institutions are prevented from realizing the importance of the adult undergraduate population across the nation because of their institutions' age-exclusive enrollment practices. Ageism's manifestations in adult enrollment patterns mean that those with the means to produce the most educational research tend to be unaware of adult students' significance. This is borne out in reviewing scholarship across fields. For example, scholars who have past or current affiliations to broad access institutions that serve markedly age-diverse populations are more likely to mention, include, or center adult students in their publications than faculty who have continuous careers at more selective universities where adult student enrollments are low.

(See Hassel [2022], Hassel and Phillips [2022], Michaud [2013], and Blaauw-Hara [2021], for example.) The stark enrollment differences nationwide between selective research universities and open-access institutions, whether public or for-profit, are amplified by neoliberal labor practices that suppress the research capacities of teaching faculty. In private for-profits and two-year colleges where adult undergraduates are concentrated at higher rates than the national average, not only are faculty generally not expected to publish, but also many are on precarious appointments under labor conditions that curtail scholarly activity. Therefore, the academics who know the most about this heterogeneous group of students largely lack the research infrastructure and working conditions that enable scholarly production commensurate with their knowledge.

Age Bias in Scholarship

The obscuring effects of institutional stratification are apparent in the disuse of age as a category of analysis in much educational research outside of the field of continuing and adult education. Reviewing literature across several fields for evidence of ageism and age-inclusivity, I ask: Is age factored into intersectional analyses of marginalized student populations? To what extent are adult students represented in scholarship about postsecondary students? In what scholarship are adult students centered, integrated, or even mentioned? In this section, I address these questions as they pertain to higher education research more broadly before combing for evidence of adult students in publications within writing studies.

The limited representation of adults in research about college students has multiple causes that reinforce each other, particularly when group characteristics and institutional factors compound. The population does differ from traditional students in ways that may discourage researchers from making them the focus of investigation. I address those briefly here and more extensively in chapter 2, in which I discuss ways to center adult students in educational research. Of more salience to this chapter's points about structural factors in adult underrepresentation, however, are disciplinary attributes that inhibit research about this group and that are related to the institutional age stratifications previously discussed. Therefore, after identifying characteristics of the group, I explain how characteristics of the discipline of writing studies have impeded an age-inclusive research agenda in that field.

Group Characteristics: Limited Time, High Mobility, Heterogeneity

Adult students' limited discretionary time, their high mobility in and out of institutions, and the group's radical heterogeneity are among the complex attributes of this group. These complexities make them simultaneously important to understand and difficult to investigate. For example, the time that adults devote to their responsibilities in and beyond academia may appear to preclude their engagement in extracurricular activities, including volunteering as research participants. The concept of "time poverty" arises from study of the severely limited time available for academics and extracurriculars when students' other nondiscretionary activities such as jobs and parenting must take priority (Wladis, Hachey, and Conway 2023). This is affirmed by researchers who engage community college student participants. They note that "our students are under enormous stress as they juggle numerous responsibilities of family, work, and school—a fact that goes a long way toward explaining why this population has evaded the kind of systematic study that we advocate" (Tinberg and Nadeau 2010, 35).

Scholars who do integrate this population into their work must contend not only with potential participants' dense schedules and overlapping responsibilities, but also with the mobility of this population. One characterization of adult learners' mobility is as a "'dipping in and out' process" (Barton 2009, 55) as such students determine when to fit college in among other responsibilities. Participants in my studies indicate that the reasons for their own college enrollment choices—about when to leave, pause, transfer, or return—are sometimes caused by dissatisfaction with an institution or their own academic performance but just as frequently are motivated by family, work, medical, and financial contingencies, often in combination. The resulting noncontinuous enrollment that is normal for this population poses an impediment to many forms of educational research. In particular, longitudinal researchers note the complications of attempting to follow participants across time, life domains, and institutions when their college pathways diverge from continuous four-year trajectories at a single institution (Sternglass 1997; Reichert Powell 2013).

The heterogeneity of the population and the variations in how it is defined may also inhibit research about them as a comprehensive group. Published rationales for terms such as "adult students," "adult learners," "independent students," and "nontraditional" or "post-traditional" students show considerable variation in the categorizing factors researchers use to define these interrelated groups. Subpopulations such as student parents may be perceived as more researchable due to having a smaller set of shared characteristics (A.F. Pearson 2019). Another subset, military veterans, may be perceived as having common professional characteristics that facilitate inquiry relevant to field-specific theories (Mallory and Downs 2014). In contrast, the broad experiential differences of the overall adult student population resist generalization. To define a research population is to place boundaries around who counts. With such a highly heterogeneous group, categorizing too broadly risks blurring important distinctions among subgroups of adult students. On the other hand, defining too narrowly risks reproducing underrepresentation of people who are already marginalized, particularly the outliers with the least conformist identities and educational histories.

Table 1.2
Articles in writing studies about or mentioning adult students

		Number of articles				
Journal	Year: volume-issue	Total	About	%	Mentions	%
College Composition and Communication	2023: 74–4, 74–3 2022: 74–2, 74.1	25	0	0	2	8.00
Composition Studies	2023: 51–1 2022: 50–3	26	0	0	1	3.85
Total		51	0	0	3	5.88

I discuss some of these considerations more fully in chapter 2 as I suggest ways for researchers to persist in their studies about and with adult students given what may appear to be daunting obstacles. The cases that I develop in chapters 3 through 5 show what is possible to learn in partnership with adult students not despite but because of their complex identities and personal histories. Although reframing these characteristics of adult students as rationales for rather than impediments to scholarship may prompt researchers to reconsider this population, long-standing patterns of disregard for adult students in scholarship across fields pose a stubborn problem because of the entrenchment of ageism.

The Slender Trace of Adult Students in Writing Studies Scholarship

Academic journals in higher education and writing studies provide evidence of a history of age disparity in research about undergraduate students. For example, a foundational content analysis of seven peer-reviewed higher education journals documents the severity of adult student underrepresentation over the thirteen-year period between 1990 and 2003 (Donaldson and Townsend 2007). Little more than 1 percent of the 3,000 articles in the review focus on adult undergraduates. That pattern of adult students' absence is evident not only in the past and in the broader field of higher education scholarship, but also in the present and inclusive of writing studies, despite the field's ethos regarding equity and justice.

Table 1.2 shows that in recent issues of both *College Composition and Communication* and *Composition Studies*, no articles center on the adult student population. This group is merely mentioned briefly in a total of three articles out of the fifty-one between the two journals. A history of inattention to adult students in this field is evident in Roozen and Lunsford's (2011) metastudy of research trends in writing studies. Their analysis covers one hundred years of journals published by the National Council of Teachers of English. Of the review's 108 citations, only three are about adult college students. The review furthermore divides writing produced in college from that produced by adults. The authors introduce the empirical studies of adult writing: "Although garnering somewhat less attention than college students, the writing done by adults did not go unexamined" (199). This frames college students and adults as two distinct kinds of participants operating in distinct scenes of writing. Such rhetorical separation of the identity of *adult* from the identity of *student* reflects the field's tacit uptake of age-segregated educational ideologies.

Structural reasons for this group's relative absence in scholarship include institutional age stratification, as I have discussed, and the nature of a discipline. For instance, to probe adult underrepresentation within writing studies, it is important to consider the field's historical focal areas. First-year writing remains a field-shaping site of research and practice. Many prominent longitudinal studies of students and their writing trace students' development starting from their entry in basic writing or first-year writing courses. These include the Harvard Study of Undergraduate Writing (see Sommers 1980), the Stanford Study of Writing (see Lunsford, Fishman, and Liew 2013), and monographs such as *Time to Know Them* (Sternglass 1997), *Persons in Process* (Herrington and Curtis 2000), *Rehearsing New Roles* (Carroll 2002), *Engaged Writers, Dynamic Disciplines* (Thaiss and Zawacki 2006), and *Retention and Resistance* (Reichert Powell 2013). Adult students, however, are absent from or minimally represented in such studies in part because they may transfer into institutions with composition course credit earned elsewhere, perhaps when they were of traditional age. Or they may opt to take a composition exam through the College-Level Examination Program (CLEP), an expedient practice often used by student veterans because it is accepted for course equivalency at many institutions. Without a noticeable presence in first-year composition courses—particularly those at research-intensive universities—this group may thus go under the radar of most writing studies' scholars.

However, a study from the 1990s offers reasons and methods for renewing research about and with this population. *Writing and Identity* (Ivanič 1998) examines the academic writing of eight "mature students" (6)—as students over the age of twenty-five are identified in the UK. It remains a widely referenced work. In the United States, Ivanič's book has been most influential for its theoretical contributions to understanding writing's role in identity formation and as a model of methodological craft. Yet Ivanič credits the unique positionality of adult students for amplifying her ability to produce conceptual work of significance beyond the researched population. She calls for further research that centers adult student writers because they are at points of critical learning:

> I suggest that mature students engaged in academic assignments provide a prime example of . . . "crucial moments of discourse". They have not had a smooth, uninterrupted path through the education system like regular undergraduates, so what is demanded of them is unlikely to 'come naturally'.

> Returning to study represents a turning-point in their lives, when other adult commitments and experiences—other social worlds—are juxtaposed with the academic world. In such circumstances they are caught up in conflicting social pressures when writing. Whatever aspect of writing we are interested in is therefore likely to be thrown into sharp focus by studying these writers. (Ivanič 1998, 5–6)

Compared to her work's lasting impact on theory and methodology in multiple fields, Ivanič's research subject—adult college students and their writing—has thus far only a slender legacy. However, recent work at the intersection of veterans and writing studies takes up this call. In *From Military to Academy: The Writing and Learning Transitions of Student-Veterans,* the author identifies Ivanič's work as the most significant model for developing theoretical findings from case studies of adult learners (Blaauw-Hara 2021). Blaauw-Hara's investigation of veterans attending community college explicitly rejects deficiency discourse about such students and related assimilationist practices that seek to make veteran students normed to their less experienced peers. He instead argues: "The massive influx of student-veterans is an opportunity for colleges to examine how many of our practices are built around the erroneous assumption that our students are rank novices, not just inexperienced with coursework, but also with life. This assumption is particularly unjust to veterans, who . . . arrive at college with highly developed senses of responsibility, a polished work ethic, wide-ranging life experiences, a history of successful learning, and practice writing in a variety of genres" (107).

His is one of a handful of books that center student veterans in writing studies research. *Writing Programs, Veterans Studies, and the Post-9/11 University* (Hart and Thompson 2020) also builds on prior work including an edited collection, *Generation Vet: Composition, Student Veterans, and the Post-9/11 University* (Doe and Langstraat 2014), and a special issue of *Kairos* on rhetoric, technology, and the military (Edwards and Hart 2010). Collectively, this scholarship positions military veteran students as important writers to study and serve. Veterans and community college students (who are sometimes overlapping populations) are exceptions to the otherwise severe underrepresentation of adult college students in rhetoric and composition research.

Despite enduring a general lack of institutional support for research, teacher-scholars like Blaauw-Hara who investigate community college writers provide some of the most age-integrative scholarship in writing studies. This does not mean that adult students are the focus of much of this work. They are not. Instead, adults tend to be included among the diverse students featured in two-year college writing studies scholarship. Another monograph and two recent collections are indicative of this practice. *Community College Writer: Exceeding Expectations* (Tinberg and Nadeau 2010) integrates adults among the student cases in a proportion close to their enrollment rates in the sector. *Two-Year College Writing Studies: Rationale and Practice for Just Teaching* (Jensen and Griffiths 2023) has one chapter focused on adult first-generation immigrant students (Suh 2023). In other chapters, authors include parents and workers in descriptions of the heterogeneous groups of students that form the community college population. The most nuanced representations of adult students are achieved in *Sixteen Teachers Teaching: Two-Year College Perspectives* (Sullivan 2020). Adult students in this volume are authors and contributors to classroom learning cultures rather than problems to be solved or, worse, inconsequential outliers of the collegiate student body. They are integrated into multiple chapters that represent the highly diverse classrooms that are characteristic of community colleges. Furthermore, all four student-authored chapters, whether written by adult students or not, discuss the importance of age-integrated classrooms for advancing all students' learning (Pierpont 2020; Rodriguez 2020; Sekscenski 2020; Stepule 2020). By engaging such students as participants and authors of educational scholarship, this collection demonstrates unusually age-inclusive approaches to research.

Several renowned literacy scholars who were adult undergraduates author scholarship that is anchored in their own educational experiences. They take critical angles on exclusionary educational ideologies and practices that marginalize students along lines of socioeconomic difference. Autoethnographic scholarship by members of the profession includes *Lives on the Boundary* (Rose 1989), *Bootstraps* (Villanueva 1993), and *PHD to PhD* (Richardson 2013). While none of their texts use adultness as the chief lens through which the authors theorize literacy and marginalization in higher education, these prominent members of the field all entered postsecondary education as adults, and they write from that positionality—as insiders and outliers to academic culture—as they examine the classist and racist systems they navigate and try to hold the field accountable for its professed commitment to equity.

My aim in *Insiders, Outliers* is to build upon the efforts of other justice-oriented scholars like these by demonstrating what can be learned through anti-ageist intersectional research about the writing of college students. My research agenda thus widens an established racial equity lens in writing studies by deliberately centering adult students across racial identities to confront age disparities in scholarship.

An Anti-Ageist Intersectional Research Equity Agenda

A regional public HBCU where one in five undergraduates are over the age of twenty-four is an apt site from which to demonstrate that race and age are jointly relevant areas to focus research equity efforts. The chapters that follow show how the heterogeneous life experiences, identities, and literate practices of adult students interact with the cultures of academia in ways that call for a radically inclusive research agenda. Chapter 2 shows that this goal can be meaningfully enacted through a range of systematic, rhizomatic, and participatory research practices. Chapters 3, 4, and 5 shift adult students from the margins to the center of academic activity by focusing on this group as writers. In these chapters, I take up Ivanič's call as I expand upon the slender but promising history of research about the writing experiences of veteran students, community college students, and other adults across postsecondary settings. Instead of examining their writing for college coursework, however, I uncover ways adult students at NCCU already are writers who have accrued rhetorical knowledge from diverse experiences outside of academia. The ethical and emotional dimensions they discuss about their writing show its capacity to fuel changes for themselves and the people and institutions that they care about. What adult students reveal about the writing they do across their life domains has powerful implications for conceptualizing writing beyond academia as we teach writing across the curriculum to students of any age.

2

Doing Research about and with Adult Students

During the research that led to this book, I discovered that normative research practices only go so far for representing the radically heterogeneous educational histories, literate practices, and rhetorical knowledge of the adult students at NCCU. Sometimes I had to let go of my assumptions about best practices so I could follow where adult students led me. The basis of the research remained anchored in standard qualitative data collection methods for interviewing adult students about their writing lives, and I used established analysis strategies to code some of the transcripts. These were fine methods up until they weren't.

In this chapter, I tell a series of methodological stories that show the research situations that prompted me to develop a rhizomatic, participatory methodology that includes both systematic and improvisational elements. In these research scenes, the more traditional practices I relied upon reached their limits, so I had to go further in order to do the work ethically. I was often slow to adapt, however. I thought I had taken sufficient pains to tailor the research design according to what I understood about the adult student population at NCCU. However, as the example situations reveal, the research cultures I am part of are not neutral, nor are the tools I use for inquiry. The same ideologies that result in exclusionary and stratified enrollment are engraved in research norms that can result in misrepresentation of adult learners. Confronting inequality in higher education means not only performing structural analysis, as I do in chapter 1, but also reflecting on individual practice. I had to face the fact that my own carefully crafted research plans sometimes reproduced the harm that my research agenda was trying to address.

Reflecting on this problem every time it resurfaced was uncomfortable but necessary. It resulted in modifications to almost every stage of research. The myriad revisions I made on the fly follow a pattern: When a research process seemed to be going sideways, I needed to release assumptions about doing things a certain way, yield to what an adult student was trying to show me, and adapt accordingly. This entailed paying attention to my emotions that signified discomfort and experimenting outside my known terrain to stretch the boundaries of research. It was hard to navigate the competing paradigms, one familiar and accepted, the other improvisational and perhaps risky. Whenever I did so, though, I was rewarded with deepened understanding of this complex group of writers. I thereby learned that the biggest risk lay in hewing too closely to my planned protocols. I had to become open.

My purposes for telling these stories are multiple. First, I seek to be transparent about how I came to the findings in the chapters that follow, especially because my approaches became atypical. Second, I need to be frank about how I am implicated in the higher education ideologies that I criticize. These research snapshots thirdly indicate, as other chapters do, some of the friction between adult learners and common practices in higher education. Finally, I hope that by disclosing my situational rationales for trying unexpected approaches, I can encourage other researchers to follow cues from their participants when a carefully wrought study of adult students does not go as intended.

What I do not offer in this chapter is a set of replicable methods for researching adult learners. That eludes standardization, just as these students do. Instead, I define and illustrate the methodology I developed during the studies that result in this book. Although traditional qualitative methods are the substrate, my descriptions emphasize the organic, relational, and situational adaptations I made at critical points when standard approaches proved harmful or incomplete.

A Systematic Substrate

I mention in the introduction to this book that my research about adult learners began with an interdisciplinary, collaborative project that asked adult students to identify factors that affected their decisions to leave, delay, and return to college. I excerpt lightly from focus groups and interviews that the student-faculty team conducted during that project. The majority of the students cited in this book are participants in a subsequent study that focused on the writing lives of adult students. The systematic substrate for the chapters that follow comes from those interviews. Thirty students were selected to approximately represent NCCU's adult student population in terms of gender and race distributions. I also sought maximum variation in age and fields of study, anticipating that variations in adult experience would follow without specifically selecting for it, such as range of employment and complexity of family responsibilities. Half of the participants are undergraduates, half graduate and professional degree students. The age floor for undergraduates is twenty-five, thirty for graduate students. (See Appendix.) Participants were interviewed using a semistructured interviewing protocol adapted from Seidman (2019) and Brandt (2015). They were asked what, how, and why they write on the job, in school, and for themselves and their communities. I conducted most of the interviews. Two adult undergraduate researchers helped with recruitment, a subset of initial interviews, and informal preliminary interpretations.

Six writers among these thirty were selected to develop more extensive cases. They participated in three or more interviews each; they collected their own writing samples, including both finished pieces and in-process works. I gathered from three to ten artifacts per writer, using these as the basis for in-depth interviews. The artifacts include writing done for classes and jobs but also several completely unexpected genres; outliers include a sidewalk chalk message written during the pandemic and choreography. I asked participants to discuss anything about their chosen artifacts and writing experiences that would help me to understand their writing lives across a breadth of activities in and outside of school. Of the thirty participants in that study, I directly cite fifteen in this book. The majority of these adult students chose to be represented by their real names. I also draw lightly from four interviews and a focus group conducted during the previous study. Most of these are anonymous or represented with pseudonyms. I mention five of the adult undergraduate research partners who have significantly contributed to my understanding about this population, two of whom were also research participants. Autoethnographic observations of my interactions with and about adult learners in classes, at campus events, and in our research partnerships augment this material.

The conventional research designs suggested by this description form the substrate for studying the educational and writing experiences of the adult learners at NCCU. To follow where these students took me, however, I also needed to adopt alternative approaches, which I discuss more extensively.

Rhizomatic Improvisations

I have known Stuart Parrish since 2013, when he took his first of several classes with me. Back then, he would arrive at 8:00 A.M. with his motorcycle helmet tucked under his arm, ready to roll from the street to a technical writing class that included dual enrolled high schoolers, residential students, and several adults who were working professionals. It wasn't just the helmet that set him apart from this age-inclusive group of learners. The same basic characteristics of gender (male), race (white), and age (over fifty) that position Stuart firmly within broad U.S. cultural norms instead mark him as a demographic outlier in the context of NCCU, where Black women in their teens and twenties comprise the largest group of undergraduates. Institutional enrollment data for 2019 show that students over fifty represent less than 2 percent, white students about 15 percent, and men less than a third of undergraduates. In spring 2019, I supervised Stuart on an independent study during which he explored interdisciplinary approaches to research on nontraditional students. He originally became interested in this topic when he was a focus group participant discussing experiences with other adult learners. As part of his independent autoethnographic field work, Stuart met with the university's diversity and inclusion director to discuss services for adult learners; he learned that student age was not generally regarded as a characteristic relevant to diversity, equity, and inclusion (DEI) activities. That new information bothered us. Why wasn't age difference part of DEI officers' mission? We knew from multiple sources including personal experience, the focus group Stuart had joined, and surveys of adult students that many struggled to experience a sense of belonging at a university that was largely structured for traditional-aged students. This moment of dissonance became a possibility for sharing findings with audiences whom I had not anticipated. Months later, I learned that NCCU would be hosting a national conference of DEI professionals. This was an opportunity to encourage DEI offices to consider an age-inclusive conception of diversity. I proposed to present about this with Stuart and Jamal Whitted, the undergraduate researcher (since graduated) who had facilitated Stuart's focus group.

One morning after the proposal had been accepted, Stuart and I met at a café to prepare for the conference. I suggested to him that the DEI audience might benefit from learning about his and Jamal's unusual educational histories. Having them discuss their idiosyncratic cases would complement the quantified survey findings about factors that contribute to adult students' decisions to delay, leave, and return to higher education.

There was a long pause while Stuart mulled this idea. Then he began drawing.

The circuitous diagram that Stuart created captures a fundamental tension between the lives of adult learners and the efficient linear ideology of higher education. He draws against the norm, transgressing the paper's rule lines as he creates long looping stretches and jagged switchbacks. On a diagonal, he marks the letters A-B-C-D to stand for the milestones of four-year academic progress, but he does not number them as years 1-2-3-4; that timeframe conflicts with his history. The straightest line he draws is a faint, fast arc through these letters. It is not Stuart's path. That fictional normative line has little to do with the realities of a first-generation college student in his late fifties who

FIGURE 2.1 Stuart Parrish's diagram of his higher education history. (Photo: C. Fulford)

has enrolled for variable periods and reasons at six different institutions, sometimes part-time, sometimes full-time. The line nevertheless haunts his drawing as the referent that his history contests.

Stuart's drawing does more than illustrate his own educational history. It exposes a broader phenomenon: the unruly organicity of many students' lived realities does "not fit neatly into established linear grand narratives" (Gravett 2021, 1506). Accordingly, a small yet provocative body of higher education scholarship, largely from outside the United States and primarily about marginalized students, utilizes Deleuze and Guattari's concept of the rhizome to resist reductive characterizations of students' college transitions (Amundsen 2022; Gravett 2021; Taylor and Harris-Evans 2018). For instance, Gravett criticizes common metaphors such as journey, pathway, and bridge that shape educational beliefs and practices. She argues that the narrow linearity these figures express elides the multiplicity of learners and misrepresents the variability of their experiences of transition into college. She and others turn to rhizomatic theory to conceptualize heterogeneity in resistance to pervasive normativity in higher education. The theory's basis in a nonhierarchical biological form, the rhizome, offers a model that is "detachable, connectable, reversable, modifiable, and has multiple entryways and exits, and its own lines of flight" (Deleuze and Guattari 1988, 21). Of particular utility for conceptualizing adults in higher education, a rhizome has capacities for growth from any point, in any direction, that can occur with "relative slowness and viscosity, or . . . acceleration and rupture" (4). In place of the efficient unidirectional progress narrative that more common educational metaphors evoke, the figure of the rhizome can account for multidirectional growth and connections, and even noncontinuity and alternative forms of persistence. Deleuze and Guattari write, "A rhizome may be broken, shattered at a given spot, but it will start up again on one of its old lines, or on new lines" (9). Theorizing diverse individuals' educational histories through this means offers a capacious approach for understanding these experiences within complex adult lives.

Deleuze and Guattari's work also suggests nonnormative methodological possibilities that are relevant to studying the adult student population. They claim that "there is no difference between what a book talks about and how it is made" (4); the heterogeneity of the adult students in my studies must be represented through methodological heterogeneity. Accordingly, I adopt a rhizomatic methodological approach by employing alternative methods in response to emerging needs during the research process. As with the scholars whose work inspires me, I see rhizomatic analysis as the core of this practice. However, rhizomaticity also applies to improvisational methods I tried when confronting limitations at other stages of the work such as recruiting participants and interviewing. Lifespan writing scholars Phillips and Dippre argue that "radical, rigorous improvisation" (2024, 7) is necessary for researchers who seek to understand the complexities of lifelong and/or lifewide writing. "[W]e use that term improvisation in its most powerful sense—an intentional, deep engagement with openness and possibility and leveraging the available resources for the most powerful outcomes" (2024, 7). As the methodological stories that follow show, my rhizomatic improvisations tend to blur distinctions between research stages and foster slippages in the traditional boundaries between researcher and researched. The point of this methodological improvisation is not to disregard the strengths of systematic practices but instead to augment them as necessary toward understanding a population comprised of outliers.

When Coding Falls Short

Although I depend upon traditional analytical methods that include quantitative analysis of educational data to contextualize the adult student population and standard qualitative coding methods to discern patterns across participants, I find rhizomatic approaches necessary to counterbalance these distancing, abstracting moves. These approaches afford possibilities for developing understanding about unusual cases, and for forging interpersonal solidarities and untidy connections across data points, narratives, and texts. For instance, when Stuart called my attention to the exclusion of age difference from the DEI matrix of student identities, that was a rhizomatic moment that launched the research in a new direction in terms of its potential audiences.

Stuart's intuitively visual approach for conceptualizing his own educational history is also an example of a rhizomatic methodological moment. Witnessing him address a research question through drawing opened me to experimenting with creative analysis techniques, especially at points in the research when more traditional methods seemed to flatten rather than deepen the findings.

Other educational researchers have likewise found that traditional coding practices alone cannot do justice to the stories and insights of marginalized, minoritized, and nontraditional students. In a study of the college transitions of twenty Indigenous Maori students, most of whom enrolled as adults, Amundsen confronts the limitations of coding for explaining "the irregularities, the messy, contradictory, chaotic and profoundly meshed, interconnected whole-of-life contexts within participants' transition stories" (2022, 1686). Similarly, Taylor and Harris-Evans report that coding's focus on reducing complexity falls short for analyzing highly variable college transition experiences, especially when nontraditional students are among the participants (2018). Within writing studies, Montes and Tusting note the tendency of hierarchical coding logics to "prevent us from taking into consideration those elements that might not fit with our previous understanding of a phenomenon or within our coding scheme" (2024, 240). To attend to such "transgressive data" (St. Pierre 1997, 175), all these researchers adopt a rhizomatic analysis methodology, following MacLure's application of Deleuze and Guattari's philosophy to develop "post-qualitative" approaches for ethnographic educational research that are "suited to, and emerging from, the situation they address" (2022, 6). The theoretical capacity of rhizomatic analysis for making sense of divergence, singularity, and irregularly as well as for crafting lateral associative connections makes it an apt approach for thinking about the nonnormativities of adult students' experiences. MacLure suggests as well that the turn toward affective openness offers a corrective to the abstract closure of coding: "Gut feelings point to the existence of embodied connections with other people, things and thoughts, that are far more complex than the static connections of coding" (2013, 172). The relationships between participants and their stories, between researchers and participants, and between researchers' stories and participants' stories can remain open and fluid with rhizomatic analysis.

A signature move made by practitioners of this approach is identification of "hotspots" (Amundsen 2022; MacLure 2013; Montes and Tusting 2024; Taylor and Harris-Evans 2018). When referred to as "data hotspots" (Taylor and Harris-Evans 2018, 1258), it may seem that the heat exists in the data itself. However, MacLure's descriptions of these research moments situate the heat both in the object of analysis and in the researcher's intensifying gaze (2010, 2013). Some detail in the record catches a researcher's attention and "connections start to fire up" (2010, 282) in a process that is simultaneously intellectual and affective. Hotspots during my analysis process usually occur while I am working with a transcript that elicits an unexpected surge of feeling-thinking. I feel moved, puzzled, distressed, jarred, delighted, curious, or in awe, and drawn into the singularity of a person's thinking about an experience, usually one that falls outside of my own. *What are you telling me? Let me pay closer attention.* As glimmers of my own ruptured or incomplete understanding, hotspots invite me to go deeper, to coax something out from that potential growth point on the rhizome.

My analytical methods typically include relistening to recordings and rereading transcripts multiple times, making corrections to these commercially prepared transcripts to ensure they reflect what participants said. Alongside this, I keep a running research journal to note anything that strikes me during these processes. I follow this by categorizing and coding excerpts in relation to my original research questions. I evaluate the yield from both open and closed thematic coding processes (Strauss and Corbin 1998; Geisler and Swartz 2019) and find these efforts are generally satisfactory for developing selected conceptual themes. However, I experienced a moment of profound discomfort during one such work session that caused me to question the ethics of overreliance on coding for my work with adult students. My doubts surfaced strongly when I was attempting a closed coding process that entailed uniformly dissecting interview transcripts into clauses as a base unit of meaning. Speech, with its pauses and tonal inflections, sometimes resists precise grammatical slicing, yet the problem for me was less technical and more about a gut feeling that surfaced as I worked with one participant's interview transcript. Transcripts are already-reduced versions of an embodied interaction between researcher and researched. They are at least two phases away from the corporeal experience of being present with another in a particular time and space, even during remote interviews. First, the audio recording strips away most sensory aspects of the occasion, then the transcript further distances the researcher from the complexities, uncertainties, and all that is unspoken during a lived encounter with another human being. My spreadsheet of decontextualized clauses was a third distancing maneuver that took me further away from the person and the meaning we had begun to make together during a co-interpretive interview. Was I doing harm to the stories, the lives, of participants when I reduced their speech to fragments and codes? Was the effort to extract and abstract, to treat the interaction as mere data, a form of dehumanization? I could not shake my feeling of unease.

I paused formal coding to see how else I might discern what participants were teaching me. The experimental methods that resulted were organic, affective efforts to pay attention to the words left behind after interviews while also recalling the personhood and contexts informing our conversation. I consulted my post-interview research journals to help identify evocative moments—"hotspots"—in the transcripts, which I then delved into using an associative slow reading and questioning practice, sometimes crafting found poems from small sections to aid my interpretive thinking (Faulkner 2020; Ohito and Nyachae 2019; Tarabochia 2024). In so doing, I indirectly followed the lead of participants. Although no one I interviewed advised me outright on how to analyze interviews (since that was not a practice in most of their repertoires), what they told me about their writing practices helped me understand that emotion and creativity can suffuse the act of writing across life domains and genres. This led me to experiment with a flexible repertoire of approaches for interpretation and analysis that made room for me to think-feel-write in response to a specific participant's insights.

Creative practices leaked into my analytic mode. Revisiting interviews with new openness might entail close reading, poetics, drawing, movement, and/or assemblage depending on what participants revealed about their practices for creating meaning. I started adopting some of their modes during my efforts to make their experiences tangible for myself. For instance, when working with one participant's remarks about choreography, a writing practice that is entirely outside of my experience, I recognized that movement and sound were vital aspects of her writing process that I rarely thought about. At first, I disregarded this example because it was so different from the others and I didn't think I had the knowledge to analyze it. Did choreography even count? But I checked myself. Tamara Vanie had specifically selected that piece to discuss with me. Why? What could I learn by sidestepping my doubts? To attempt to get closer to Tamara's ways of knowing, I queued the music for the dance she had choreographed, "Lovely Day" by Bill Withers, then let that wash over me on repeat as I reread her choreography notes and the transcript about why and how she drafted the dance. I released my usual constrained writing posture to gesture in ways that were suggested by the participant's descriptions of writing choreography with her whole body. This opened me to a fuller understanding of the importance of movement, both physical and metaphorical, in this adult student's writing life, a realization that I further unpack in chapter 3. Through such open approaches to other transcripts and their rhizomatic possibilities, I moved my way back into each interview, revisiting areas that snagged my attention, noticing where participants' specialized knowledge eclipsed mine, and riffing associatively on their observations and insights about writing to forge connections that were unavailable to me from the distance of standard coding procedures.

Rhizomatic Listening

MacLure and the ethnographic researchers of transition who have taken up rhizomatic methodologies do not explicitly discuss its applicability for addressing cultural differences between researcher and researched. However, practitioners' openness to uncertainty and discomfort and their emphasis on connection and affect resonate with practices of rhetorical listening that are salient for conducting interviews across differences (Ratcliff 2005; Rosenberg 2015; Royster 1996). Although my identity as a former adult undergraduate provides a potential point of relatability with participants, other aspects of my identity can interfere with building the trust that enables interpersonal research to go deep. For instance, my roles as faculty and researcher mark institutional power distances from students and participants, and my whiteness is a nonneutral cultural difference from the Black students who are most of the adult learners at NCCU. To take a rhetorical listening stance for interviews with them means being conscious of reasons for distance or distrust that I may or may not be able to reduce yet trying to anyway by centering participants even when this takes me off a planned trajectory. As conscious as I try to be about this rhizomatic process of yielding, unexamined privilege and dominant beliefs about research can seep into my practice, resulting in missteps that can be hard to resolve.

My research journal about an interview with one participant and her family illustrates emotional dimensions of attempting to establish an open, listening stance while butting up against my own limiting beliefs about research processes. It also shows that a genuinely participant-centered approach applies not only during the interview itself but also in research actions that surround the interview.

May 23, 2018. Research journal.

> Chanel was scheduled to interview yesterday, but she missed her 6:00 P.M. appointment. I called her at 6:20 and learned she was at soccer practice with her daughter. She had totally forgotten. I offered to reschedule. She asked about location (she's an online student) and if it was ok to bring her daughter. At first I said no, but then I realized it was important to recognize the logistics that parents and online students deal with. . . . When I confirmed Chanel's rescheduled appointment, I wrote this:
>
> "If you aren't able to easily make other arrangements for your child, and you think she can entertain herself pretty well for about half an hour, I'm open to having her join us. Thanks for asking about that. It's real!"
>
> I'm glad I was flexible, but I wondered if she would show up. . . . I was feeling a little cranky. The AC was out in our building and my office was in disarray. . . . When my phone rang at 6:00, I was sure Chanel was cancelling. No! She was just asking for precise directions from the car. I could hear her young daughter in the background.
>
> Stepping off the elevator were not only Chanel and her seven-year-old daughter, but also a man about Chanel's age. Chanel and the man were in matching hospital scrubs. I offered papers and markers and sticky notes and a nearby classroom for overflow, but they all seemed to want to be in my office together. We made it work, and Chanel volunteered that her companion would be good to interview as well. (John[1] was an online student at NCCU, too.)

My initial misgivings about having a child in the room while interviewing Chanel derived from prioritizing planned systematicity over emergent situational and relational needs. I assumed there was something sacred about having each other's full attention. How would we be able to concentrate? And what about confidentiality? What would the institutional review board have to say about this scenario? It took stepping back from this reaction for me to try to imagine the situation from the mother's perspective so I could release my own assumptions about what mattered most.

When I relisten to that recording, I hear the accompaniment to our voices. A little girl's hair beads click in the fan's breeze as she sits in her mother's lap. When Chanel drove out of her way to share her perspective with me, I thought that sharing would be just through her words, but it was through her actions, too. Adjusting my protocol to welcome her family resulted in an unorthodox interview setup. Yet the unexpected benefits of accommodating a participant's schedule, responsibilities, and relationships went beyond merely salvaging a missed interview. I gained tangible evidence of the primacy of parenting in many adult HBCU students' lives. I also would not have interviewed John without Chanel's introduction. He had even more to say in response to the interview questions than Chanel had. Perhaps this was because he had heard each question and his partner's responses already, so he had more time to think through his answers.

From this encounter, I developed a new orientation toward my methods and my relationships with participants. Previously, I had interpreted my training in qualitative research ethics and reliability to require methodical adherence to data collection protocols. Consistency mattered, didn't it? But interviews are not data, they are events in people's busy lives. The consistency I sought was not legible to Chanel and John, for whom this interview was a one-off. They helped me think more situationally. I learned to follow participants' lead and to trust them to participate on their terms.

Other researchers challenge normative methodologies when these prevent underrepresented populations from participating in research; they recommend adopting approaches that center the realities of the population being investigated (Price and Kerschbaum 2016). I learned this on the fly, clumsily, and it proved especially important when interviewing Black mothers whose time and attention were often divided. To participate, they sometimes needed something other than what I had envisioned when I planned the study. For example, I had designed some accommodative flexibility into the protocol by allowing participants to choose either in-person, phone, or video interviews. When I called one of the women who had requested a phone interview, she was in the midst of driving carpool. I offered to call at another time when she was free, but she said no, this was as free as it got. We spoke over the ambient sounds of traffic and children, pausing during her exchanges with other families as she let her riders out. It was as ethnographic as a remote interview could be. I had to rethink my expectations about one-on-one undivided attention, a commodity in short supply for many adult students at NCCU, especially Black working mothers. The more I learned about their lives, the more I realized what generosity these students extended when they followed through on research participation, whether it went as I had planned or not.

The flexibility that is necessary given the realities of adult students' schedules is more than an accommodation, however. Because it has the potential to engender findings that could not otherwise happen, flexibility as an investigative strategy manifests in openness to the unplanned that can yield unexpected data, relationships, and conceptual development. For example, meeting John and Chanel together cracked open my thinking about the roles of intimate partners and other family members in the academic and writing lives of adult students. I had not initially been looking for that. Even though I should know better by now, even though my field has long asserted that writing and learning are social processes, the individual remains the default focus of inquiry for much interview-based research. Per the study's approved protocol, I continued conducting one-to-one interviews, yet meeting Chanel's family attuned me when other participants spoke about how their partners, spouses, and children—and grandchildren, parents, grandparents, siblings, cousins, and chosen family—were entwined in their literacy experiences in and out of school.

Demonstrating an open stance while learning from adult students is critical for establishing trust during the research process. As Chanel's case shows, parents and other adult students may have constraints on participation that a researcher can accommodate; being flexible is important when attempting to represent a population that typically has overflowing schedules that can change suddenly due to myriad responsibilities. Openness also pertains to leaning into the semi part of semistructured interviewing by attending closely, noticing where participants place weight, and yielding to topics raised by them. It means slowing down to inquire deeply rather than rushing to the next prepared question. This relational form of open attention enabled me to learn more than I was expecting and to exceed my own disciplinary preconceptions. For example, my protocol included questions about adult students' experiences of difficulty with writing. Given my disciplinary reading about transfer theory, genre theory, and discourse communities, I anticipated responses about participants' difficulty with writing in unfamiliar professional or academic genres. When many participants instead led me into areas of difficulty that were about grappling with ethical and emotional dimensions of their writing, it was important for me to set aside my disciplinary frameworks and ask more about these situations so I could learn something I did not already know.

This situational methodology helps me learn more than I could have planned from students like Stuart and Chanel. It is informed by literacy scholars who have developed robust ethnographic co-inquiry practices with adult writers. (See Ivanič 1998; Roozen and Erickson 2017; Tarabochia 2021). Rosenberg and I discuss the feminist genealogy of co-inquiry and its applicability for lifespan writing researchers (Fulford and Rosenberg 2024). We argue for yielding to participants' expertise about their own lives when jointly interpreting their writing and learning experiences. In a chapter coauthored with participant-collaborators in our respective research projects, we further show that in cultivating these relationships over time, we have blurred the roles of researcher and researched in ways that strengthen our capacities to make meaning together (Rosenberg, Fulford, McGowan, and Long 2024).

Critical Collaborations

This book was informed by collaborations with many adult students that took multiple forms ranging from approaching interviews as co-interpretive events to engaging adult undergraduates as research partners, to working in solidarity with a student organization. In fact, most of the scholarly work that I did at NCCU was in collaborations with colleagues and students who were stakeholders of the institutional issues we studied together. As I discuss in chapter 1, this research was constrained by the high teaching and service responsibilities that are typical of faculty workloads at HBCUs and other teaching-mission institutions. Yet the university did support these sorts of projects. My first study of adult learners, for instance, was conducted with an interdisciplinary team of faculty and adult undergraduates to learn about the stories behind this group's enrollment patterns. We were internally funded through Academic Affairs, which sought collaborative proposals that addressed issues pertinent to the university's strategic plan. As insiders, the student investigators on the team contributed to recruitment, led focus groups of their peers, and helped faculty investigators tease out salient initial findings. Investigating in such close consultation with members of the researched population opened up crucial lines of trust and experiential breadth, as I have written elsewhere (Fulford 2022; Wymer, Fulford, Baskerville, and Washington 2012). Furthermore, working across our different institutional, cultural, and experiential standpoints sparked insights that would not have been possible in solo work, particularly solo work conducted by a white researcher about students at a historically Black institution.

Despite my immersion in collaborative practices, I briefly muted this commitment to participatory research when I sought funding to launch a new study of adult students' writing lives. I applied for residential humanities fellowships at two institutions in hopes of carving out time to extend the scope of my studies of adult learners. I felt the need to describe my research agenda in terms that would be legible to reviewers at more prestigious organizations. While the fellowships I sought actively recruited applicants from minority-serving institutions, the research values embedded in their application processes aligned with the solo scholarship norms of more elite traditions. I confess that I savored the idea of time and resources to develop a new study on my own, a year for working independently on data collection and analysis, separated from my usually abundant teaching, mentoring, and program administration responsibilities. It was a seductive vision. But it was not the right model for this study.

Fortunately, once I secured external funding, this normative fantasy of myself as the solitary humanities scholar began unraveling. Even before the fellowship started, I shifted back to a collaborative paradigm because of an unexpected encounter at the summer DEI conference where Stuart, Jamal, and I presented. It did not occur to me that I might meet adult NCCU students or alumni there other than my co-presenters. I was surprised to be greeted by the MVP from a recent technical writing course, Yaseen Abdul-Malik. A history major, Yaseen had been an energetic presence in the class despite a life overflowing with commitments outside of school. On the first day of Yaseen's class, I had asked students to estimate the time they devoted to nonacademic responsibilities so we could discuss these in relation to the coursework. Although a majority reported that they had jobs and extracurriculars, Yaseen's response was especially striking. He estimated that between his newborn and two jobs, he routinely clocked ninety hours a week of responsibilities beyond his full-time academic load. During the semester, Yaseen often arrived a little late to class because he was rushing from work. Once or twice, he wheeled in with his tiny son because his wife was a working student, too. Yet he always showed up in body, mind, and spirit, and it was my favorite class that semester in no small part because of Yaseen's infectious desire to learn.

Yaseen was not at the DEI conference as an attendee. He was volunteering. He needed to earn service hours toward graduation, and he had not been able to fit them in during the school year. NCCU has a community engagement classification from Carnegie, and the university requires full-time undergraduates to perform fifteen hours of service each semester. Even when they care very much about civic engagement, working parents like Yaseen are significantly challenged to meet this requirement on the university's terms. Yaseen mentioned that he was still trying to find ways to satisfy the service hours in time to graduate in December. I immediately thought, well, why not bring him on as a research intern? The strengths he showed in class might prove beneficial to my next project. Perhaps we could arrange an internship through my department so Yaseen could earn academic credit and service hours simultaneously while contributing his insider perspective to the research.

When I broached this possibility with the internship coordinator at NCCU, she agreed; then she asked me about taking on another adult student who was seeking an internship, too. Thomas Kelly was a self-employed carpenter and former restaurant manager who was taking classes part-time toward an interdisciplinary studies degree. It wasn't about the service hours for him; he was interested in being involved in interview research because he was considering a career change to counseling. But I felt ambivalent about this request. Yaseen was one thing, but Thomas was an unknown. What would he bring? What would he need from me? Would my hard-won research year turn into a mentoring year?

After Thomas's academic advisor assured me that I would not be disappointed, I relaxed into teamwork mode, my native habitat. Thus Yaseen, Thomas, and I set in motion a study I had briefly, erroneously, envisioned as a solo project. They became my thinking partners at key points in the early months of the research. We altered my recruitment and interview protocols to better reach their peers, and they conducted some of the initial interviews with individuals who appear in this book. Their relatability to other adult students and their professional experiences in sales and service were especially beneficial during this startup phase. For instance, although I sent our cowritten recruitment emails through the offices of Veterans Affairs, Transfer Services, and NCCU Online, direct peer-to-peer recruiting was an effective supplement.

Their most memorable recruitment event was a social held at our Transfer Services office. The director had invited me, but I could not attend. Thomas and Yaseen took charge instead. Yaseen needed to bring his baby. This turned out to be a bonus for recruitment. (There is no better magnet for people's attention, and other parents could relate.) The two men described the study about adult students' writing lives and signed up potential participants. Afterward, Thomas urged me to be in touch with one of the new transfer students, Adrienne Long. She was rallying students to form an organization so they could advocate for themselves and have a place to belong on campus. He described her as passionate about the same things that motivated me. This was an excellent lead. Adrienne subsequently became not only a participant, but also a champion for the entire adult student research agenda, and then a coresearcher herself. We became entwined in each other's projects because the values that drove her to establish a campus organization for adult learners aligned with my reasons for doing research about and with them.

This cascade of interpersonal and rhizomatic connections was sparked originally from Stuart's participation in a focus group facilitated by Jamal, then getting involved in research about adult learners himself. His interest in stretching the parameters of DEI to be more inclusive of adults put us at the conference where I reconnected with Yaseen. Asking about internship options for Yaseen led to Thomas, who conducted the first interview with Adrienne. Adrienne's sustained involvement sparked additional ripples of connection.

For instance, Adrienne welcomed me to planning meetings about the nascent adult student organization as she and other students met to share their experiences and determine a way forward. Mainly, students and their children were at these meetings. Adrienne invited other campus personnel, however, because she was building a network of support for the student group. She gave us space to discuss what we were doing on campus that pertained to adult learners. This provided me with an opportunity to discuss the research about adult students with the population that it was about, as it unfolded.

My second time visiting this group was in the wake of a disconcerting research problem. In the acknowledgements to *Writing and Identity,* Ivanič quotes her colleague, Dick Allwright, who advises researchers: "If you have a problem, share it with your readers" (1998 xii). To this, I add: "If you have a problem, share it with the people your research is about." I went back to the adult student group after my team's initial rounds of recruitment to report that we had solid numbers of people interested in being interviewed, but I was distressed about who was missing. Black men in their twenties and thirties were severely underrepresented so far. I could not ethically go forward with a study that replicated the wider culture's neglect of this population. Could they help? Many at the meeting offered to spread the word to men who might fit the parameters of the study.

One young man volunteered on the spot. Gary Lassiter said he had heard about the study before, but because he was not a parent and was only financially responsible for himself, he figured that he did not meet the criteria. He knew other students with way more family responsibilities. Once he heard about the ramifications of my recruitment problem, though, Gary offered to be interviewed immediately. We tucked into a corner of a nearby office to talk after the meeting. What he said deeply affected me. Although we only met that one time, I returned repeatedly to the recording over several years of analysis, identifying different hotspots to dwell on as he taught me about lifewide writing. I had designed my study to potentially investigate learning transfer by peering into what I treated as distinct domains of writing—personal, work, community, and school. Gary steered me in another direction: "I feel like all of my writing is for myself, everything. I don't separate it like, 'This is school writing, and this is my writing.'" Gary's holistic perspective on his professional writing experiences at a call center and day care inform discussion about the ethics of writing on the job in chapter 4. His insights about rewriting traumatic experiences are the seed for a theory of writing as a mode of emotional agency that I develop in chapter 5. Perhaps the most significant thing Gary taught me, though, was to be alert to continuity in other participants' writing experiences. Just as Chanel taught me to pay attention to the roles of family in adult students' educational and writing experiences, Gary taught me to string together hotspots within individual interviews so I could detect concepts that apply to a participant's writing as a whole. For instance, the case of Tamara Vanie that I discuss in chapter 3 is informed primarily by Tamara, of course, but I also credit Gary with teaching me to interpret her interviews holistically, to ask what connects her disparate writing experiences.

I could have stuck to coding. I could have excluded outlier genres. I could have rejected participants who couldn't give their full attention. I could have privileged my own expertise about writing. I could have run the study solo. I could have kept the problems to myself. Dippre and Phillips argue, however, against methodological rigidity. They note that the complexities of research on lifewide writing "force change, adaptation, and improvisations" (2024, 375). The methodological scenes I have shared from the field reveal that I often struggled to recognize the right thing to do when normative research moves interfered with my ability to learn from adult students, thus my reliance on a rhizomatic and collaborative methodology, too.

There are many reasons to trust the systematic research methods that have been honed by many researchers over time, and these do form the substrate for my work. However, they are not universally appropriate for accessing the nuanced knowledge of students who have divergent educational and writing histories. Through discomfiting research situations that did not fit the spreadsheet or the protocol or my own disciplinary assumptions, I eventually found my guiding principle: When in doubt, center the students.

3

Rewriting Persistence

In chapter 1, I examine ageism in higher education as it is manifested in enrollment stratification and underrepresentation of adult students in scholarship. That analysis shows the national, regional, and disciplinary terrain in which adult college students remain ambiguously positioned as both insiders and outliers. They are a vexingly heterogeneous population in a postsecondary sector that is largely designed as an age monoculture even when adults are a strong demographic presence. This is the quantitative and ideological backdrop to the narratives that follow about adult students at North Carolina Central University. Their stories humanize the numbers with their specific educational histories and their radically diverse lifewide writing experiences. In the remaining chapters, an ensemble of adult undergraduates and graduate and professional degree students share perspectives on writing. In this chapter, I center one adult undergraduate's case to test normative constructions of education and writing against the granular evidence from her writing life.

Tamara Vanie is a veteran and a married Black mother of five whose attainment of an associate's degree took sixteen years over four states and five institutions. At first glance, Tamara and Stuart Parrish, the NCCU undergraduate whom I briefly profile in chapter 2, seem to have little in common. Stuart is a white male civilian musician in his fifties with no children, a lifelong North Carolina resident. Yet Stuart's and Tamara's educational histories share a pattern that is not uncommon with adult learners: multiple schools, many attempts, long stretches when school was not their focus, and an abundance of reasons that a fast four-year pathway did not map onto their lives.

Before examining her writing experiences, I contrast Tamara's circuitous educational history with the normative academic definition of persistence, and I offer an alternative that better accounts for adult students like her. The need for a broader concept becomes apparent when I focus on even one adult learner rather than higher education systems in analysis of educational trajectories.

"I've Been Trying to Get There Forever"

Tamara's higher education history exemplifies episodic—and epic—persistence toward degree attainment that is not uncommon for students who have multiple adult responsibilities. While her college experience is unique in its specific choreography of moves, it nevertheless represents the realities of many adults who must factor in family roles, employment, relocation, illness, disposition, support, and other fluctuating life conditions when they make decisions about how, when, and whether to continue their studies. These conditions are largely absent from models of persistence and retention that dominate higher education rhetoric about students' degree progression. Continuous linear educational progress is privileged in the measurement culture of postsecondary education. The prevailing model of persistence excludes the nuanced understanding of adult students like Tamara.

The National Student Clearinghouse Research Center (NSCRC) defines "persistence" per its usage in institutional research: "Persistence rate is measured by the percentage of students who return to college at any institution for their second year, while retention rate is by the percentage of students who return to the same institution" (Gardner 2022, 1). Persistence's partner term, "retention," is thus a subset of the persistence rate; it measures three-semester enrollment duration for full-time students who remain at the same school (NCES 2022b; NSCRC 2023). These standard definitions used by NSCRC and other research bodies like the National Center for Educational Statistics (NCES) are quantitative, aggregated, and limited to first-time, full-time students (NCES 2022b). These metrics guide much institutional research because they are tethered to higher education funding and ratings. The ubiquity of this exceedingly narrow quantitative way of conceptualizing persistence has all but erased qualitative usage of the term in higher education discourse, and it is part of the set of dominant practices that continue to marginalize adult learners that I criticize in chapter 1. I therefore advocate for recovering the qualitative and holistic dimensions of persistence to include adult students and their decisions about where to apply their energies at a given period of their lives. These individuals may or may not start a second year of study immediately after their first. Their "first year" of college may or may not consist of a full academic year of credit. Adult students nevertheless are persisting when they retry college repeatedly after necessary pauses and when they attend part-time over time to accommodate schooling alongside their other responsibilities and goals. Even when they are not enrolled, adult learners are likely to be persisting in a logical course of action, including learning outside of formal education. To address limitations in the dominant usage of "persistence" within higher education discourse, I use the verb or gerund forms, "persist" and "persisting," and I lean into a more common definition, "to continue . . . despite opposition, setback, or failure."[1] The common meaning encompasses all that adults persist through, not only in their academic lives.

Tamara's educational history illustrates how this alternative concept of persisting applies to her educational progress despite a pattern of episodic enrollment. It also applies to her writing life, as shown through several situations that she identifies as meaningful cases of nonacademic writing: pregnancy, dance, entrepreneurship, and activism. As the examples demonstrate, the writing practices she uses and the rhetorical knowledge she deploys help Tamara move in and across these disparate sites of activity, all of which she describes as "socially driven." Collectively, her stories frame a new understanding of writing as a means of persisting through difficulties and resisting injustice. I borrow her term, "creating movement," to think about situations when Tamara uses writing to enable herself to persist (move through) or resist (move against) in these situations. I also analyze Tamara's use of the word "try," which occurs frequently when she describes her repeated efforts to attend college and to create other kinds of movement in her life and her community, including choreography, business and nonprofit development, and educational activism.

Tamara Vanie started straight out of high school at a community college in Kentucky that expelled her after her first year, "probably because I was like out fighting people." A second-chance semester at a different community college campus "didn't work out." At no point in her many tries at college would she have been regarded as persistent per the standard quantitative definition. But her willingness to keep trying over time means she *did* persist with education, albeit not continuously. Additional college tries included brief enrollment at a for-profit institution and, later, at a private nonprofit's branch campus on a military base. Meanwhile, she persisted in other life domains. She married, divorced, and remarried her husband after reconciliation. She joined and reenlisted in the Army. She endured two miscarriages and birthed five children including twins, and she and her family moved multiple times across Kentucky, Texas, New Mexico, and North Carolina. In 2005 when her first baby was not yet a year old, Tamara made her third college attempt at an institution "where they kind of get you through quick." The advertised speed to a degree did not materialize, however. Tamara succinctly explains the interlocking parenting, marriage, and economic trials that had to take priority over school at that time: "I had life situations happen where I was trying to find care for my daughter and go to class at night and work. And my husband, we had kind of broke up by this time. . . . Trying to deal with that made it hard to go to class, so I end up dropping out of that school. And me and my husband reconciled. . . . Trying to save my marriage, I was like, I need to do something to help us work out. What can I do? So I decided to join the Army."

"Trying" surfaces in this excerpt three times. Tamara tries to find childcare. She tries to cope with her marriage ending. Then she tries to "help us work out" by enlisting. Across her many interview transcripts, Tamara utters the verbs "try," "tried," or "trying" a total of fifty-eight times. About her journaling, she says, "There's a sense of self that I'm always trying to practice." About choreography, "There's a video of me trying to work through it." The most frequent phrases are about learning, such as "trying to see," "trying to understand," "trying to figure out," or "trying to work through." She also layers the verb in rapid succession when listing her efforts to go back to school: "[I] tried after she was born, I think. I tried to go back to school, she was maybe like ten months. That was 2005. I tried to go back to school but this time didn't go to a community college."

Persisting as trying does not always mean continuous action toward goals. Sometimes threats to continuity require pausing more than once. Two years after dropping out of the "get you through quick" program, Tamara enrolled part-time at a campus on her military base, "but of course, mission first, and the Army doesn't always care about your classes when they have missions and goals they have to do, so [I] failed those classes, had to withdraw." This was Tamara's fourth significant setback to completing a college degree.

While Tamara was enlisted, her ability to determine her own priorities was deferred due to the primary duties she had to the Army. On the one hand, the military improved her access to higher education by providing educational benefits and a branch campus on base, yet this employer's "mission-first" priorities proved an insurmountable conflict with Tamara's college goals at the time. It was seven more years before Tamara tried college again after she was no longer enlisted. This time, her marriage was stable, the family was settled, and military benefits enabled her to enroll at a third community college where she "just kept going." This was her fifth try to earn an associate's degree. Her educational narrative continued to be punctuated by changes at home and work, yet she persisted. "I did start school at that point, in early 2014. . . . Got pregnant. Stayed in school. Had my son in October, the fall semester of my first year. . . . I kept going to Durham Tech, just kept going using my VA benefits, post 9/11. Had another son. Oh, started working. I started working for a nonprofit that serves women and children here in Durham. Moved my sister in with her three kids, so I had eight kids in my house at this time. Had a fifth baby in 2017. Then I graduated from Durham Tech in 2018. . . . And here I am . . . at Central . . . finally. I've been trying to get there forever."

Tamara's higher education narrative portrays movement and recursive effort as she persists in ways that the mainstream educational definition of "persistence" does not address. A roomier definition, however, makes space for pauses, gaps, and returns. She leaves college multiple times, but she also returns. She demonstrates a form of persistence that is more than staying power on one set course. It has the quality of returning after a change, returning after reconsideration, persisting as a form of drafting and revising that applies across life domains. Tamara tries marriage when she is expecting her first child. It does not work the first time. She and her husband divorce, reconcile, and retry using different approaches. Tamara's enlistment in the Army, for instance, is an attempt to mitigate financial stressors that were among the difficulties during their first years as a married couple. A similar pattern of tries and retries applies to college. Tamara attempts multiple forms of college at different points in her life. Her many retries represent persisting by approaching the elusive goal of a degree from different angles, with revised purposes, and under different conditions. The conditions Tamara had created for her last four years at a public two-year college enabled her to finally make steady progress on an educational goal that took sixteen years across five institutions.

Given the prevalence of adult students like Tamara, it is absurd to refer to community colleges as two-year institutions and the associate's as a two-year degree. The standard higher education nomenclature of "first year students," "four-year degree," and "four-year institution" are also misnomers that elide the normalcy of students engaging in education part-time or episodically. These fixed-term phrases for a nonfixed experience contribute to adult students' erroneous positioning as outsiders in academia.

If we read Tamara's movement in and out of college from a higher education enrollment standpoint, her status would have been categorized as "some college, no degree" during each of the periods she was not enrolled (Shapiro et al. 2019). The nomenclature that the NSCRC uses has since been revised to "some college, no credential" to account for certificates and other nondegree credentials (Causey et al. 2023). Within this large population (36 million adults in 2019, 39 million in 2023), the NSCRC identifies a group of most interest to college recruiters—the 10 percent whom they identify as "potential completers." These are individuals who, per several predictive measures, are most likely to successfully complete a college credential (Shapiro et al. 2019, 4). Prior to enrolling at Durham Tech, Tamara would not have been categorized as a potential completer due to her age, the length of her nonenrollment, and the low number of credits she had accumulated at multiple institutions. According to these standardizing terms, Tamara's achievement of an associate's degree is unexpected given that only one in five of those who re-enroll after a seven-year gap in schooling go on to earn a college credential (Shapiro et al. 2019, 10). Falling outside of the potential completer category implies that students with educational backgrounds like hers need not be a priority for recruitment, programming, support, or any of the investments that institutions make in their students because their odds of attaining a degree are deemed low. However, Tamara did become a degree completer, and more than once.[2] Her case furthermore suggests that those who do not appear to be potential completers may face more structural barriers to returning to school than those who are regarded as potential completers.

There are many people like Tamara who could be regarded instead as core constituents of higher education in the United States. To make that change would require revising assumptions about what academic track records tell us about student potential. We might also interrogate what constitutes credentials for aspiring students who have not yet earned degrees. As I further demonstrate in analysis of her writing life, Tamara developed public rhetorical credence as a Black mother and activist even before earning her first academic credentials. In her community, she accrued experiential authority that she used to advocate for people and institutions that mattered to her. This kind of learning, influence, and persistence that occurs outside of academia is difficult to capture in standard measures of academic achievement. Institutions that offer portfolio assessments of prior learning attempt to do so.[3] Helping adult students translate their existing knowledge into credit units facilitates their degree progression and demonstrates respect for this population, but there remains potential for deeper integration of adult students' prior knowledge into academic life. Tamara's and other participants' stories encourage me to imagine what higher education would look like if it were infused with the knowledge and experiential authority that adult students bring to their studies.

Tamara's life from high school graduation through earning her first college credential appears precarious and inconsistent when interpreted through a conventional higher education lens. It is laced with struggle. Her first four college attempts resulted in expulsion, failure, and withdrawal. Analysis of longitudinal data on degree attainment indicates that such "nomadic multi-institutional attendance behavior increasingly known as 'swirling,' [holds] a significant and negative relationship to degree completion" (Adelman 2006, xxi).[4] These terms, "nomadic" and "swirling," carry negative connotations similar to the terms "drop out" and "stop out," which are also used in foundational literature about retention and persistence to describe students who leave college before completing a degree (Tinto 2012). From extensive work with marginalized students, however, Barton argues for describing noncontinuous educational pathways from such students' perspective as an ongoing process of "dipping in and out" (2009, 57). This framing is a better match for Tamara's characterization of her repeated college attempts.

Centering the person instead of centering the system of higher education enables a more holistic understanding of Tamara's powers. A portrait of intellectual and creative growth and social contribution emerges when the focus is on Tamara as a mother and wife, a dancer and choreographer, a military service member and social entrepreneur, and a community activist. Being a student is an important strand of Tamara's life that she returns to repeatedly, but it is only one strand among many. Unfortunately, the continuity of Tamara's adult life while she dips in and out of higher education is illegible from standard quantitative measures of postsecondary persistence. It is therefore important to study students like Tamara to offer a corrective to the limitations of quantitative measures. Those with academic trajectories that defy normative expectations expand the ways it is possible to think about postsecondary education, whom it serves, and options for more flexibly integrating students' knowledge gained through family and personal life, work, and community activity.

Researchers of academic persistence tend to regard adults' outside commitments as "risk factors" to degree completion (NCES 2015). Some mark normal life activities of employment, childcare, and household work as the most labor-intensive nondiscretionary activities that compete for adult students' time. These responsibilities are cited as contributors to "time poverty," in which time available for academics is reduced in proportion to time required for other activities (Wladis, Hachey, and Conway 2023). Considering risk factors and competition for time may help account for some of the periods Tamara had to dip out of college, but the words "risk" and "poverty" contribute to deficits discourse about what adult students lack. This discourse is misaligned with adult students' experiential abundance, as Tamara's case exemplifies. Furthermore, the segregation of academics from other sites of experience contradicts participants' characterizations of priorities and connections across their multiple responsibilities and interests, including those that educational researchers regard as nondiscretionary and discretionary. During our co-interpretive investigation of Tamara's writing life outside of academics, she pointed me to samples from areas that might be regarded as discretionary yet are essential to her. These include her personal writing, entrepreneurial efforts, and activism, which I discuss in depth in this chapter.

"Creating Movement" with Writing

Tamara writes constantly. She writes "in the living room, the kitchen table, . . . our study, . . . in my room, the porch." She writes in the car while her daughter has dance lessons. On her phone and in a bound journal, she keeps notes about whatever she's reading or the next new business or nonprofit she has in mind. Tamara writes to keep pace with her abundant ideas. The majority of what she writes is for thinking and learning or as a scaffold for speaking and creating. Writing is often about getting her thoughts down in preparation for action. She takes elaborately coded reading notes, and she uses writing to synthesize her thinking across different areas of knowledge. These kinds of writing support her efforts to teach others such as in homeschooling and church groups, and in her public speaking as an activist for educational equity. She also overflows with ideas about business and nonprofit development in service to the Black community.

Writing is part of a repertoire of practices she uses to persist through and resist pervasive racism, sexism, and other challenges to her vision for herself and the people and institutions she cares about. In the sections that follow, I analyze four examples of Tamara's writing that illustrate its value as a vehicle for persisting and resisting. First, briefly, I show how her practice of personal journal writing contributes to Tamara's ability to persist through illness. Then, through analysis of her choreography, I suggest how writing can be used as a tool for liberatory self-development that resists restrictive roles for women. In a third example, I show how she uses writing to facilitate her family's foray into social entrepreneurship in an industry in which barriers to gender and racial economic equity are entrenched. The fourth example looks at writing as scaffolding for Tamara's agency as an educational activist. Tamara regards all these as interrelated; her core values about social justice drive each of these activities, and writing is a way of putting those values into motion.

"Something for Me"

As a mother and active community member, Tamara gives of herself abundantly, yet she also attends to her own needs and interests. Writing is part of that. She journals. She keeps elaborate reading notes as she teaches herself hydroponic gardening. She brainstorms ideas for new projects, and she choreographs. She names these activities "development of the person." In these efforts, she is simultaneously creating herself and resisting ideologies of womanhood that she finds too restrictive. She comments during an interview: "There's a sense of self that I'm always trying to practice, especially because I'm only thirty-six and I have five kids. So I'm always like, 'Okay, mothering is something that I do. And I am a mother. But who is Tamara?' So this is me trying to . . . I don't know. It's confusing, but trying to do things that are just me . . . just Tamara and not mom, or wife, or anything like that. But just developing . . . the person. So that's why it seems like I always have a lot going on in my life. I want to do something for me, too. You know?"

Among her writing practices for self-development is a journal she began during her pregnancy with twins when she was coping with medical complications. "My husband bought me a journal because I was just in a bad mood all the time. He was like, 'You need to write, you know, write down how you're feeling and how you're getting through this,' and that's when I first started writing." Journaling starts as a means for persisting and moving through the hardships of that pregnancy; the material practice of handwritten journaling persists beyond that period. She explains why: "It's something for me. It's not for anybody else. I do a lot of stuff that's for every fricking body else and it's kind of like the one thing nobody can get in the way of, you know? And it takes care of me and promotes self-awareness." The practices she developed during her pregnancy are evident in other kinds of writing for which she uses a bound journal, such as her personal reading notes. She says, "I wouldn't mind doing six, eight, ten pages of notes because to me, that's easier than carrying around a whole big book. If I'm studying you know, I keep reading through the same stuff. . . . I don't do it for my classes as much, but . . . I use it for my personal reading."

The portability of a journal facilitates Tamara's movement from place to place in an extremely full life of parenting, school, community activity, and work. Her bullet journal contains elaborate reading notes about hydroponic gardening that she studies out of her own interest, business planning that she does with her husband, and choreography that she writes for her own self-development.

Like her personal journaling, Tamara's choreography is "not for anybody else," and it facilitates movement even more literally than her journaling. She has been dancing for her whole life and choreographing dance and cheer routines since high school. "My body understands it, and it's like second nature," she says. A recent development in her lifelong practice is learning to create dances through a "choreography by chance" method, an improvisational composing process that was pioneered by modern dance icon Merce Cunningham.[5] Tamara took a workshop on the method, then she experimented with it to create new combinations of movements. She drafts a long, numbered list of possible moves from her repertoire, rolls dice to select from these moves to create a chance sequence, "then I turn the music on and start working through it." She describes these chance procedures: "There's really no rhyme or reason to it; it's just whatever comes out, and then you put those sequences together, which become phrases, and you do those specific moves. You can apply it to all dance forms."

Aptly, Tamara's process of composing dance incorporates movement, sound, and video while she drafts, although not necessarily all at once. Beyond the pen-to-page movement of handwriting is the physicality of throwing dice to invent sequences. Tamara tries each move as she assigns it. "Without the music, I would create a [move] and practice it," she says. Then she would play the song while testing, with her whole body, the full sequence of choreographed moves, adding repetitions and adjusting the performance tempo to work with the music.

Choreographic composing requires space in ways that I do not usually associate with writing. When I think of writing as embodied, I picture small motor movement: fingers on keyboard or phone, or a pen gripped in my dominant hand scratching away at the margins of a draft. The typical scene of writing is equally small in my mind, just the immediate surfaces, rarely larger than a desk. I think of large movements such as walking or stretching as breaks from writing. Tamara's choreographic practice upends my thinking. With her first roll of the dice, Tamara's whole-body drafting approach deviates from the typical smallness of writing movements and spaces. Her "working through" stage requires even larger motions and spaces as she tests every aspect of the dance she has written. In contrast to her journaling that "nobody can get in the way of," her choreography is more interruptible because of its spatial requirements: "There's a video of me trying to work through it, what I wrote, but my kids were just getting in the way. . . . I was recording myself working through and then I was like, 'I'll just try it later. They're not going to let me do this right now.'"

Children may interrupt Tamara's expressive self-development, but family is also a source of inspiration. An emotion-inflected memory of her grandmother prompted Tamara to create a new dance using the choreography by chance procedure: "Bill Withers had just died, and he wrote "Lovely Day." I was like, "Aw, man. I grew up with that song," because my Oma, . . . I just remember her always playing that song because she had one tape she would always play in the car, so we all knew these songs really well. . . . I was really sad about him dying, but then I was like, "Wow, this was a good memory for me, hearing the song . . . with my grandma," so I wrote that choreography for it."

The dance movements Tamara creates through her composing practices serve a liberatory function, as she explains: "[My] choreography is socially driven." That's the same phrase she uses to describe what connects all her writing. In the case of choreography and dance, the socially driven motivator is "about women's rights and identity and roles," she says. Her choreography thus entails two kinds of movement, the embodied movement of the dances she creates and the feminist movement that defends Tamara's right to move as she pleases in resistance to structural sexism. Tamara desires unrestricted movement as a woman in which the expression of her dancer identity exists alongside her identity as a mother without contradiction. Yet she acknowledges tension between her confidence in her dances and her awareness of others' judgments. "Me doing a heels dance on my own I'm still nervous about, although I know I could create it." She envisions going public with her dances, and she keeps a video dance diary, which she says she plans to post "when I finally get to the point where I'm like, 'It's okay to put this out there' and be okay with scrutiny."

Critical voices are not far from the surface when Tamara talks about dance. She worries not so much about the quality of her work but instead about critics policing her freedom of movement as a mother. The words "nervous" and "shouldn't" come up repeatedly as she invokes those who may question her on the grounds of respectability: "I'm just nervous because a lot of people don't know because it tends to be a little more sensual, and then it's like, 'Oh, you're

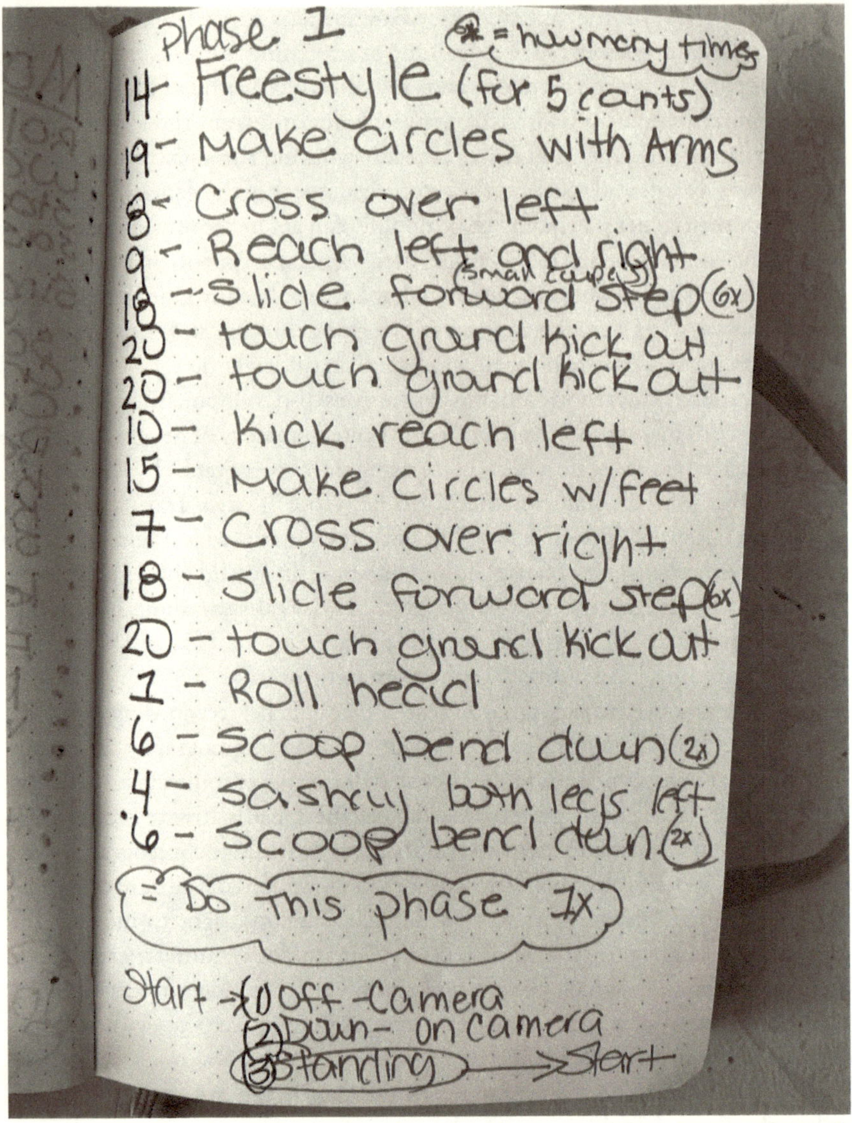

FIGURE 3.1 Tamara Vanie's choreography by chance for "Lovely Day," by Bill Withers. (Photo: T. Vanie)

this mom. Why are you doing that?'. . . . But that is who I am. I like doing heels class and I like doing hip-hop, and I am a mom and I have five kids. To see me move like you would move in a heels class or even in a hip-hop class where you're shaking and gyrating, some people may be like, 'Oh, you shouldn't be doing that, you're not teaching your kids right.'" The shouldn'ts seem to be forces that she pushes against as she asserts and reasserts her right, through composing and performing, to express her identity beyond rigid conceptions of mother and wife. "Like, 'Oh, because you're in the mother role and the stay-at-home wife role, you shouldn't do this.' So I'm going to go do that because that's actually who I am and I'm not going to go pretend to be somebody I'm not anymore." Here are repetitions of "who I am" as Tamara persistently invokes her full identity in resistance to respectability discourses. She continues her improvisational composing method and sensual dance practice despite feeling that she is being judged.

Performance of a dance may be ephemeral, even private. But through choreography and recorded dance diaries, Tamara asserts the potential for a public identity as a woman who creates emancipatory movement outside normative boundaries of motherhood.

"We Want to Humanize the Trucking Industry"

In the same bullet journal where she writes choreography, Tamara takes research notes about the trucking industry and sketches business plans. Through these writings, Tamara rehearses ways she might intertwine the industrial movement of trucks and drivers with the social movements that drive her actions: Black economic justice and gender equity. She and her husband David explore the possibility of developing a sustainable family business enterprise that resists replicating the unjust employment practices that are common in the industry. Tamara retains her commitment to gender and racial economic equity while trying to figure out how to accomplish their family's economic goals. Writing is a prominent tool in the repertoire of practices that she uses to form her social entrepreneurial ideas. Her entrepreneurial writings include plans she and David make for developing two family-run businesses: a trucking company and a dispatching service to route the trucks.

Figure 3.2 shows a task list for launching the dispatching service, The People's Logistics. The business name hints at Tamara's democratic vision for whom the company will serve. Just as she understands dance within broader social constructs about women's roles, Tamara sees entrepreneurial activity as a way to address problems that are simultaneously personal and systemic. Her father and husband are both long-haul drivers. Her lifelong proximity to the industry informs her critical perspective on the impact of business practices on employees and their families. She describes her and David's priority: "We want to humanize the trucking industry, because it's very not." Humanizing starts with respecting drivers' family responsibilities beyond their financial contribution: "The goal is to build a relationship and build trust with the drivers so that they know our dispatchers are really, actually trying to get you home, and we're trying to keep organized, and be the most efficient we can. Because we know your time with family's important, too." Her emphasis on trust and the family-forward, people-centered bottom line informs the

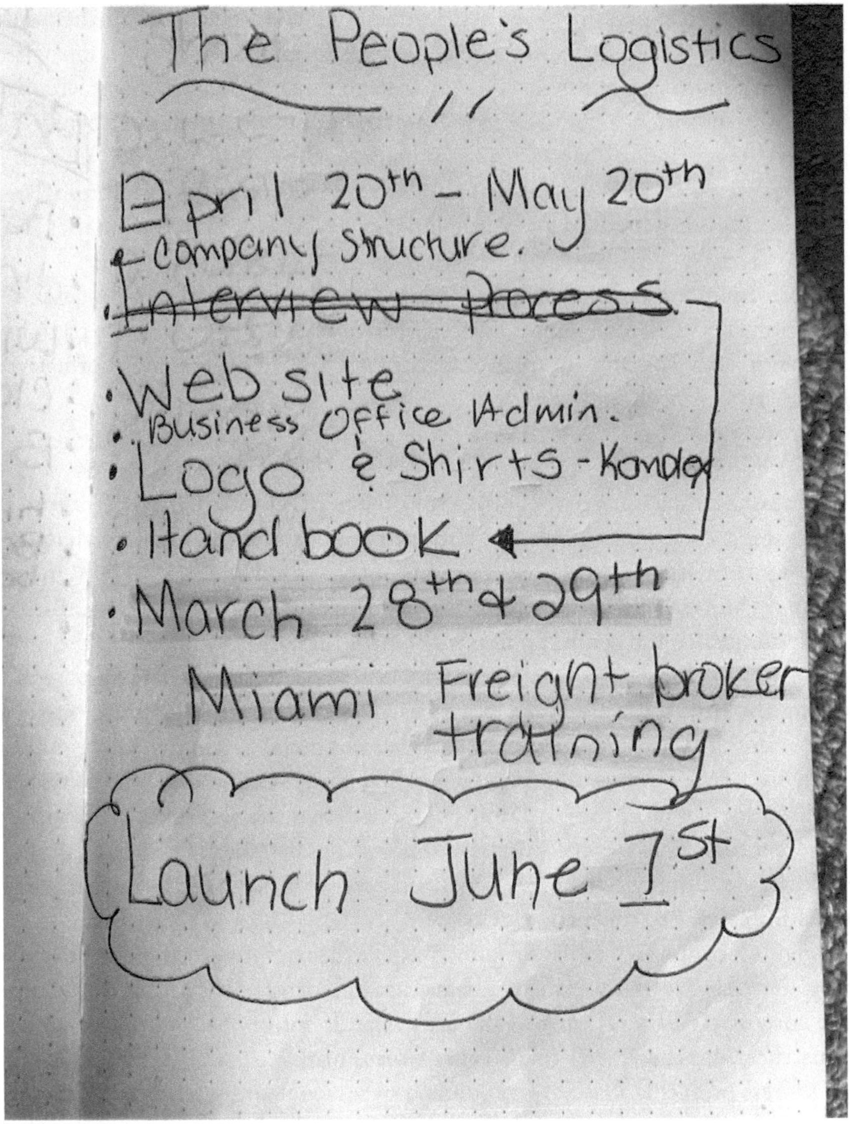

FIGURE 3.2 Tamara Vanie's planning list for a trucking dispatch service, The People's Logistics. (Photo: T. Vanie)

business names they draft: Need Trust for the trucking company and The People's Logistics for the dispatching service.

Building generational wealth in Black families that have historically been economically marginalized is another layer of the Vanies' values-driven venture. Tamara situates their family's planned enterprise squarely within traditions of Black social entrepreneurship: "The business asset is about Black business owners, family legacy, how to set your kids up, and how to help our community, because the trucking company we're hoping will do that, too. Provide jobs. Felons are out here driving trucks for way under what they should be, but they have to because no one else will hire them, right? So they deserve to be paid what they're owed."

This statement makes evident that Tamara's social values extend beyond benefits to her own family. Tamara and her husband David discuss ways to be equitable employers in an industry known for being "exploitative and dangerous" (Balay 2018, 185). Tamara wants to extend their social impact to include equitable treatment of women, but she knows this runs against the grain of trucking culture: "How do we address the fact we do want equality in this very male dominant atmosphere, and then build it? . . . How do we protect women that work for us and hold other men in the space accountable for how they do women that are in the industry? But that's going to be tough." Culture change won't be easy, yet Tamara persists in foregrounding gender equity while planning the social mission of the family enterprise.

The Vanies use a highly collaborative approach to the learning, thinking, and writing necessary for developing these conjoined businesses. Learning from each other's perspectives on the industry enables them to cocreate their vision. She says, "when my husband and I sat down, . . . we're like, "Look, trucking needs to be more family friendly. I want our trucking business to be more humanized." Tamara and David augment their ideals and experiential knowledge by studying industry-specific business development practices and seeking advice from other Black social entrepreneurs. For example, Tamara explains: "My brother-in-law brought us this book . . . on trucking . . . [that] talks about the whole business and how it's structured. . . . . So I started to think about it for Need Trust, and I wrote that out. . . . I jotted some ideas down there, too, about how I wanted the structure." These jottings represent a complex learning process by which Tamara builds up her business literacies, synthesizing new material with her existing values and knowledge. Writing threads through every phase of the process.

Industry-specific research is not sufficient for the Vanies' knowledge base because of their social equity aims. They seek to also learn from Black entrepreneurs outside of trucking who could help them fuse practical business considerations with their ideals. The owner of a local community-oriented coffee shop offers guidance in this arena. "He's like, 'Yeah, look. I have this consulting business . . . and I could really help you guys in bridging the social aspect of your company to the economic side.'" The Vanies meet with him for feedback as they draft their plans, demonstrating her practical knowledge about writing as a social process that benefits from seeking and using input. Tamara's approach to developing an employee handbook is also informed by readers. Because she has consulted handbooks as an employee herself and observed clients' expectations of a social services handbook at one of her jobs, Tamara decides that employees will be involved in revisions to their trucking company's handbook: "The next two to three drivers we hire will get it and read it. We'll definitely get some real feedback, then." She does not use the terminology of user testing, yet Tamara employs a user-centered approach to drafting materials for imagined future employees. Her repeated efforts to seek and use feedback furthermore indicate that she is well aware of writing as a social and recursive process that can take many iterations to get right.

Academics typically evaluate students' writing itself, not what the writing accomplishes or enables. Grading norms position writing as the fixed end of a process. Alternative grading schemes may honor the process of producing writing, but Tamara points to different ways of thinking about writing. It is somewhere in the thick of a process that has other ends besides a "finished" written artifact and other means woven into the effort alongside the writing. In short, writing is not an end but a means. The act of writing helps her put principled action into motion. For instance, choreography yields dance, which is an assertion of her freedom to move. Writing business plans also generates principled action because it is intended to improve family life and Black economic mobility with extended social impact into the community. In the analysis that follows, I examine how Tamara's activist writing serves as a means for moving past fear to express her own stance within a collective resistance movement.

"To Change the Culture of Education"

In Tamara's community work, she further expresses the socially driven values that are a common thread across her writing life. She resists racism and sexism not only in dance and entrepreneurship, but also in her jobs at social service agencies, through her involvement at church and in nonprofits, and in educational activism. Among these multiple community-oriented activities, Tamara describes a fraught period when advocates for local control of public education fought a state takeover of the school the Vanies' children attended. During this period, which was prior to Tamara completing an associate's degree, she emerges as a spokesperson for Black children and public education. Her rhetorical activity over several weeks of organizing and protest vividly exemplifies adult development of experiential authority outside of postsecondary education. It also shows writing's function in resistance work.

I provide an overview of the struggle over school control and Tamara's activist role in it through rhetorical analysis of regional media coverage during eleven days in October 2017. I also examine Tamara's efforts to manage her rhetorical leverage as a Black mother who is frequently cited in regional media about resistance to the school takeover. Her activist writing facilitates her ability to persist through struggles that are emotional and ideological. Writing also functions as a rehearsal space for speaking in resistance to systemic racism. Her activist writing involves a recursive social process that includes drafting and consulting as she hones her message and its delivery. In a high-stakes situation, she developed a public statement derived from experiential authority that walks the line between personal perspective and solidarity. The act of drafting contributes to her ability to speak up courageously, "from the heart," she says, despite her fear of public speaking and the anguish of wrangling ideological differences within the coalition of activists. The notes function like her choreography in that they guide her movement and expression in a public space. This time it is with her voice as well as her body.

In the Media Spotlight. Glenn Elementary School is less than a mile from the Vanies' home in East Durham. Their kids attend it. Of Glenn's 350 students, over 90 percent are Black or Latine (Childress 2017). Tamara refers to Glenn as "the forgotten school" because it had not received much local attention until it was flagged for a controversial statewide program. The North Carolina Innovative School District (NCISD) was part of a Republican-led plan to take over underperforming public schools such as Glenn and offer contracts to charter school companies to run them. The initial list under scrutiny included forty-eight schools comprised of the lowest-performing 5 percent across the state. Glenn was on the short list (Hui and Childress 2017). The local school board and the teachers' union rallied to retain local control. Tamara and her husband David joined the intense local resistance to this privatization. "[We] had to say something because we were the only parents really speaking up for Glenn," Tamara explained. The Vanies became the most frequently cited parents in media coverage of community response to the plan. Tamara's demeanor in the press gives no indication of how difficult the role of spokesperson was for her. The most immediate challenge she faced was a lack of confidence in her public voice. "I was terrified actually of public speaking, I really hate [it]. . . . I'll hear my voice and think I sound stupid or what I'm saying is stupid, but it's really me struggling . . . and not feeling confident in how it sounds . . . saying the words that I wrote."

Nevertheless, Tamara embodies courage and a sense of civic duty that is identified with Black women's rhetoric. "Black women internalize a conception of *kairos* that teaches them to see themselves as active agents within their spheres of influence who must act despite risk" (Carey 2020, 277). Furthermore, taking a principled stance that includes enlightening audiences about Black families' experiences with racist educational structures situates Tamara in the company of other "Black women [who] negotiate, navigate, and use their unique positionalities to make and distribute knowledge across diverse spaces and audiences" (Browdy 2021, 1). The means by which she does so are the subject of this section.

Finding her footing as a spokesperson for public education was not easy, yet the power of Tamara's words and her delivery of them in the public sphere is evident in how they are taken up in the media. From October 2 to October 13, 2017, Tamara is quoted, paraphrased, photographed, and/or filmed in at least six stories reported in five different news outlets regarding the state's controversial plan to privatize Glenn Elementary School (Alvarez 2017; Childress 2017; Hiu and Childress 2017; Philip 2017a; Philip 2017b; Sweat 2017). Reporters embed Tamara's phrasing in headlines like "Durham Parents Feel 'Taken Over' by School Takeover Process" (Philip 2017b) and "Durham School Escapes Possible State Takeover: Parent Calls Decision 'a Win-Win'" (Childress 2017). Tamara's credibility as an involved parent is emphasized: "Tamara Vanie, the mother of two students at Glenn, said community activism and unity paid off for Glenn. 'I am so pumped,' Vanie said. 'It shows what a community can do when it comes together'" (Childress 2017). The portrait of Tamara that emerges from multiple news sources like this is a highly active parent working in solidarity with the school board, teachers, and other parents to defend the school her kids attend. Tamara's support for teachers at Glenn is featured: "Tamara said the teachers at Glenn help students grow in ways that can't be measured by test scores. 'They're helping kids become adults. . . . . These teachers are facing a lot'" (Philip 2017a). Tamara's emphasis on teaching quality beyond the curriculum contrasts with the state's quantitative indictment of students' low test scores, a measure they use to justify the takeover scheme. Her nimble shift away from the state's one-note framing of Glenn as a failing school to a more compelling counternarrative about highly committed teachers in a high-need area is one of the rhetorical moves necessary to the resistance coalition as they try to move the public narrative about this school from underperforming to underresourced.

Tamara's authority as a Black parent is also utilized by the news media in images and video clips that show her speaking up for Glenn Elementary. Over the eleven-day course of the most intensive news coverage, these images visually express steadfastness and solidarity. Such qualities are exemplified in a photo of Tamara speaking at a rally in front of the school (Philip 2017a). The rally included teachers, staff, parents and children from the district, and a state senator. (See Figure 3.3.)

This coalition saved the school from privatization. The fierce local resistance at Glenn and other schools resulted in only one school in the state being taken over. The charter program was shuttered five years later (Schlemmer 2022).

Asserting a Black Parent Standpoint. The successful resistance, including Tamara's role in rallying parents and speaking publicly about educational issues, is impressive. However, two years after the win, Tamara could still recall the internal conflict she experienced between adhering to a unified coalition platform and directly addressing systemic racism in the schools. She characterizes the struggle as "finding the words to write that are true to myself and what I see as the actual

FIGURE 3.3 Tamara Vanie speaking at Glenn Elementary School. (Photo: Lisa Philip/WUNC)

issue, but then still supporting a system that I want to change in order to help my kids' school." She indicated that calls for solidarity sometimes threatened to erase or commodify her Black parent identity, a risk recognized by Black standpoint theorists (Reynolds 2002). Although Tamara agreed that school privatization was unacceptable, she felt that resisting a charter takeover was insufficient without addressing long-standing educational inequities affecting Black children and their families. Writing and talking through her ideas to prepare for public speaking helped her move through this difficult compromise.

Preparatory notes for Tamara's speech at the school rally indicate that she decided to "speak from the heart" that day, framing her contribution "as a parent and especially a black person."[6] With this phrase, she identifies for listeners the standpoint that informs her experiential authority and activist orientation. In alliance with the teachers' union and school board, she did speak in resistance to the threatened takeover. Yet she also spoke frankly about the disproportionate scrutiny of Black families and the persistent "marginalization of schools like mine" in an effort to keep the alliance focused on addressing systemic racism in the schools, a problem that requires enduring work beyond the antiprivatization fight.

In her notes, Tamara's advocacy for the "necessary sacrifice" of a day of closure in protest of privatization comes with acknowledgment of the surveillance Black and Latine parents endure for any actions they take regarding their children's education. She invokes the disparaging voice of the state as it casts judgment on the school and the families it serves: "What's so special about Glenn can't be much look at their scores," she writes, then explains, "We have been working to change that perspective and that narrative." The organizing, rallies, and press coverage of community support for the teachers and the school are all part of that effort, and all are defensive maneuvers because "as a predominately black and brown school we had to prove our worth." Tamara's speech is designed to educate her listeners about the systemic racism that undergirds the state's tendency to blame families and communities for educational outcomes. She places the one-day closure decision within that context: "Now here we are trying to decide if school should be closed or not and now I as a parent and especially a black person have to consider what does this mean for me personally, my child . . . when school shuts down and the state turns around and says again 'now Glenn your back on the list why haven't you done anything, don't take that day off your students couldn't afford that see look what you did.'"

Employing the language of sacrifice and liberation, Tamara elevates the discourse about the resistance to privatization into the language of the Black freedom movement, characterizing the one-day shutdown in protest as a message. Tamara associates abstract ideals of "liberation," "justice," and "social change" with concrete aspects of the message: "shutting the schools down," "resources for our teachers," and "equip our students." Tamara's choreographed rhetorical moves speak to diverse audiences, including those following the news coverage and those she was in solidarity with but who needed some education about the long game of racial justice. "Let me let you peer into the black struggle for a second," she says, signaling for all tuning in to notice her framing of the struggle as racial and for white listeners in particular to pay attention. In her closing, she reinforces the need "to change the culture of education in Durham" that transcends the immediate moment. Because the struggle must be ongoing, she closes her speech: "Let's continue to mobilize and build up our schools." Days later, after Glenn is removed from the takeover list, she reiterates the need to continue working for culture change when she is quoted in the press: "We're going to celebrate today and roll up our sleeves and go back to work tomorrow" (Childress 2017).

Educational disparities were on Tamara's mind as she wrestled with the responsibility of speaking up for Glenn Elementary while also holding the school system accountable for what and how they teach Black children. In discussing what prompted her to speak as she did about the educational issues, Tamara expresses concern over the persistent mismeasure of Black children. For instance, she criticizes classifying majority-Black Glenn Elementary as underperforming when that is based on "end-of-year testing [that] fits white culture. It doesn't fit Black culture." She voices the state's negative narrative about Black students: "They're saying, 'You don't know anything,' or 'You're behind,' but that may not be true." Tamara also reflected on differentiating her stance as a Black mother from that of a white friend, a teachers' union leader, as she was preparing her remarks for the rally at the school: "He was wanting to articulate more of a 'Durham for all,' so not making it about color. You know like 'All kids need this, even Latino kids.' . . . I wanted to be able to focus on the Blackness of this because that's what I know." Tamara insisted on speaking from a Black parent standpoint. She did not feel right about representing all families. "I didn't think it was fair to speak on what Latino families at my school needed because I know their culture's different from mine and I know people . . . outside of Blackness that do stuff to me, I'm like, 'Yeah, we really don't need that,' but then you just force it on me anyway because you think I need that or my community needs that *when I'm telling you what we need*. I didn't want to do that to them."

Because she knows the harm done when those outside her culture act on assumptions about her community's needs, she makes a space for other standpoints. She argues that parents from outside her culture have the experiential expertise to know what their children and families need, too. She says, "I'd rather be at the table with them and have someone there that is creating movement for what they need themselves. . . . . so that we're providing what our kids need in the same space."

Tamara is aware that her individual perspective is informed by the collective experience of Black families; she feels authorized to speak from and for this position. That she understands hers to be a partial perspective and thus seeks the participation of those from other cultures is a profound enactment of Black feminist standpoint theory in which "each group becomes better able to consider other groups' standpoints without relinquishing the uniqueness of its own standpoint or suppressing other groups' partial perspectives" (Collins 2000, 270). Tamara accordingly insists that writing and speaking while creating collective movement should be motivated from an individual's knowledge base, that "uniqueness of . . . standpoint" that Collins writes about, rather than from an organization's set of talking points. Tamara chose to speak directly from the perspective and power she has as a Black mother. This stance enabled her to specifically address issues of inequitable education for Black children while simultaneously acknowledging the value of other standpoints, including those of white teachers and Latino parents. This was her means for creating shared resistance to privatization of the school while persisting toward more enduring educational justice.

Like the outlier qualities of Tamara's educational history, the examples of socially driven writing and rhetorical situations that are discussed in this chapter defy simple classification into genres, discourses, or processes. These situations and Tamara's responses to them instead suggest possibilities for writing to contribute to resisting systemic oppression that arises across life domains. As my analysis indicates, her approaches to writing as a form of resistance can be understood through Black feminist thought, particularly standpoint theory, intersectionality, and their manifestations in Black women's rhetorical theory. For example, when Tamara reflects on her writing, and sometimes even in her writing, she readily calls up the oppressive voices that she endures as a Black woman. These include those who would scrutinize her sensual dance practice, those who would question the roles of women in the trucking industry, those who would denigrate Black children's intelligence, and those who would leave race out of discussions of local control for education. This voicing practice is helpful for concretizing the racism and sexism that she pushes against in her rhetorical efforts. Tamara's ability to perform solidarity while asserting a distinctive standpoint within a coalition is an act of nuanced double resistance that exceeds simply identifying an opposing perspective and arguing persuasively against it. This was an astute insider/outlier maneuver with which Tamara worked inside the coalition to resist the immediate threat of school takeover while also functioning as an outlier within the coalition who resisted subsuming the fight for educational quality and relevance for Black students to the fight to retain local control.

In her attempts to address sexism in the trucking industry, Tamara also occupied both insider and marginalized positions. She had insider knowledge through her lifelong proximity to the business as the daughter and wife of drivers. However, her sex and the fact that she was not a trucker positioned her outside the industry's cultural norms. She turned marginal perspective into a critical vantage point from which she could envision movement toward a more egalitarian variant in her family's business. Attempting from the margins to illuminate, alter, and occupy the center is another instantiation of Black feminist power (Collins 2000; hooks 2000). Collins writes that centering one marginalized group does not decenter others, but instead offers a way to "question whether what has been taken to be true can stand the test of alternative ways of validating truth" (2000, 271).

This captures my hopes for centering adult students in this book. With each case, I ask how prevailing assumptions about higher education, students, and writing stand up to the lived experiences of adult students. Tamara's writing life calls into question normative academic preoccupations about writing as an end in itself, instead showing it to be a vital means for putting principled action into motion. Seeing writing from this angle, as a means for resistance, opens possibilities for rethinking writing pedagogies and curricula.

Finally, Tamara's case shows that adult life blurs demarcations between essential and nonessential activities outside of academics. This is evidenced in her dance practice and community activism. She regards these as necessities for "developing the self." They are not extras. Age-integrated education calls for rethinking adult students' concurrent commitments not as impediments to academics that contribute to "time poverty" but instead as akin to the school-sponsored extracurriculars, service learning, and internship experiences that are institutionally recognized ways of achieving holistic learning. Adult students like Tamara are already engaged in their own self-sponsored development of experiential authority and their own explorations of possible selves. They are already serving their communities, already putting theories into practice. The challenge in higher education is in recognizing diverse learners' highly varied life experiences in order to place such activity in conversation with their academic lives.

4

Writers at Work

Negotiating Ethical Agency

On a rainy afternoon during the second year of the Great Recession, I started a unit about procedural writing in my undergraduate technical writing class. As the rationale, I told my students that being able to write guides, manuals, handbooks, and other instructional genres has the potential to transform an employee from mere worker to trainer. I claimed that instructional writing has value not only for the writer's employer but also for the writer because it can lead to material changes in their work life such as raises and promotions. To substantiate my claim, I told a story from early in my prior career about a time I had moved up two pay grades as a direct result of being able to write manufacturing protocols. These documents demonstrated to my boss that I could not only perform the job but also train others. I suggested that learning to write training materials, like the ones assigned in this class, might similarly help them advance their careers.

One student looked skeptical. "It doesn't always work like that," she said. Sandra[1] was a Black woman of about my age who recently had been laid off from an office manager position. I was taken aback by her remark, so I asked her to say more. She explained that she had done exactly what I advocated. She had written a handbook and trained another employee, only to have that person chosen over her for promotion. She was tired of this. Her work products only seemed to benefit other people. Sandra explained that she was back in college to credential up. She was willing to learn more about writing on her way to the degree, but she was already familiar with many of the workplace genres the course emphasized, and, for her, they were not the ticket to career progression that I claimed them to be. Sandra's forthrightness let me see the limitations of my own assumptions about writing as an uncomplicated mechanism for getting ahead. I had not been thinking critically enough about the confluence of racism, ageism, sexism, and credentialism as these permeate the working lives of the students I taught.

Years later, during my first research project about adult students, another experienced Black professional woman corroborated Sandra's experience of having her professional writing be undervalued. More precisely, Celinda Bailey's comprehensive skill set was valued at her workplace, yet the fact that it disproportionately benefited management rather than resulting in career advancement for her was a problem. She explained that she had worked for many years in county and city government without significant promotion. The sharp contrast between the pay and respect afforded her and that of the managers who benefited from her expertise was especially irksome to her:

> No matter how you look at it, that's just the way society is. Sometimes, people can graduate and not have a bit of sense, but because they have a degree, it makes a difference. I have a high skill set, but I didn't have the paperwork to follow up, so I ended up doing a lot of the work of people ahead of me who . . . were actually kind of chasing themselves not knowing how to do certain jobs. But they had the paperwork to say that they had the managerial skill set.
>
> It was frustrating, and a lot of jobs got put on me which were managerial positions, but the credit was always given to the [other] person. . . . . [My work] has promoted them and made them look good. . . . I have actually produced the paperwork, did the accounting figures, performed the budgets, did the grant writing. I have all those skills, but I didn't have the paperwork to follow up with it.

Celinda contrasts her own proficiency in the absence of college credentials to the trope of the "educated fool" (Smitherman 1994, p. 104); she finds the work world predictable but lacking in the ways it consistently rewards the latter. As insiders to professional life, Sandra and Celinda have accrued significant writing and rhetorical experience. They also have critical thinking abilities that include the capacity to detect ethical lapses at their workplaces. They and students like them provide valuable real-world correctives to oversimplified notions about careers and what professional writing can accomplish for the individuals who produce it. Sandra's intervention in my lesson also calls into question common assumptions that most students are on a college-to-career trajectory and will thus initially learn about professional genres and workplace cultures in school as part of career-ready curricula. This common educational paradigm elides the actual chronologies of movement between work and school that adult students navigate.

Higher education largely operates as if the flow of knowledge is one way: knowledge is introduced in college to be applied and further developed in professional life after graduation. This ideology is not new. The first colonial American colleges were designed as training sites for clergy, with education for professions including law, teaching, and medicine also among the earliest curriculums (Thelin 2019). The current manifestation of higher education as professional preparation is evident in the common phrases "from school to work," "college to career," and "career readiness," which circulate in the wider culture as well as within colleges and universities. Even institutions that enroll high numbers of working adult students use rhetoric that figures college as a precursor to employment because it justifies students', parents', and taxpayers' investment. For instance, colleagues who teach at community colleges tell me that "workforce readiness" is the prevailing mission at these institutions. At NCCU, this discourse is ever present in campus communications. Career readiness and market readiness are touted in the university's posters, events, and planning documents. The recurring market-ready ideology at the institutional and system level is further represented in curriculum and pedagogies that narrowly cast the directional flow of knowledge from college to the working world.

The fifteen adult students who contribute to this chapter demonstrate the radical limitations of this school-to-work paradigm. When the direction of school-to-work is inverted, or when career and college coexist, as they must for many students, one site does not prepare learners for the other. Adult students' workforce experiences often influence their decisions about enrolling in college, as they seek credentials for promotion or new bodies of knowledge to make career changes; however, their on-the-job subject area expertise and knowledge about writing, rhetoric, and ethics may or may not be recognized as assets in academic contexts. They should be. All working students have the potential to contribute field-tested wisdom that advances the understanding of their classmates and faculty. Even their experiences in relatively constrained writing environments such as entry-level office work can provide windows into workplace writing situations that exceed the curriculum. Students who have more career experience such as in education, cybersecurity, government, banking, and medical systems draw upon even more complex rhetorical knowledge while they work toward undergraduate, graduate, and professional degrees. In turn, under adult-inclusive conditions, coursework can provide opportunities for experienced professionals to resee their work experiences in relation to disciplinary concepts and values. Academic and professional life thus have underrealized potential to become reciprocal sites of learning.

Professionals and Students

The adult students in this chapter enact dual identities as professionals and students. Academic classifications of graduate, undergraduate, senior, junior, and so on are self-referential institutional categories that are largely unconnected to the existing knowledge, skill, and professional status of adult learners. In terms of workforce experience, a forty-year-old undergraduate psychology student may have more in common with a forty-year-old law student than with classmates in their programs who are two decades younger. The more experienced among such students hold positions characterized by expertise, authority, and responsibility to others. Such professional identities are at odds with higher education's positioning of students—including graduate and professional degree students—as novices who are in training to assume future roles. This chapter therefore incorporates knowledge about writing on the job as discussed by graduate, professional, and undergraduate students who were pursuing degrees in law, counseling, public administration, pharmaceutical sciences, psychology, and interdisciplinary social sciences at the time of their interviews. With ages ranging from thirty to fifty-six, they reflect accrued knowledge from diverse work histories that are as nonlinear as their educational trajectories. In keeping with broader findings about job and career change trends (Sullivan and Ariss 2021; Sullivan and Baruch 2009; U.S. Bureau of Labor Statistics 2015), these adult students' employment histories entail multiple transitions including periods of unemployment, and upward, lateral, and downward mobility across job types in response to labor market changes and life factors. Many juggle work and school simultaneously; others choose one over the other at different periods in their lives.

Their rhetorical expertise is evident when they explain the writing they do in the small businesses, large corporations, and state institutions they work for. These adult students have much to teach about professional writing and rhetoric that goes beyond basic understandings of process, audience, genre, and style. On the job, they have also had to develop rhetorical savvy about how a text functions within an institutional ecology and beyond. Furthermore, to write at and as work, they routinely negotiate power relationships in organizational hierarchies. They sort through ethical dilemmas to gauge their own decisions about what, how, why, and even whether to write. These adults learn to take responsibility for their writing and its consequences yet also to yield ownership of it in environments where their word is rarely the last. They understand that writing is not a neutral skill. Writing well has value, but that value does not always benefit the writers; adult students with professional lives know that writing well will not save them from racism, sexism, and other oppressions that are as endemic in workplaces as they are across society, yet writing can be part of their ethical interventions into these persistent problems.

What working adult writers already know is what is hardest to teach about writing in any field; that is how writing on the job actually works, and how those who do it negotiate the ethical complexities of the rhetorical environments in which their writing circulates.

Ethical Agency in Workplace Writing

Workplaces are critical sites of writing where ethical complexities abound. Brandt establishes that "when people write for pay, they must grapple as a matter of routine with difficult questions surrounding writing as contractual labor, including matters of ownership, ethical responsibility, and accountability, control, and consequence..... [T]hese questions can infiltrate even the most mundane writing tasks, engaging workaday writers in ethical and compositional deliberations of the hardest kinds as they put their minds and language into authoring texts that they do not own but for which they feel responsible" (Brandt 2015, 13). Brandt's attention to the ethical aspects of writing on the job points to the possibility of considering some of the writing performed by working adult students as acts of ethical agency even in contexts that delimit their autonomy. These are the writing situations that I focus on in this chapter.

Ethical dimensions of workplace writing emerged as a prominent theme when I asked adult students about the writing they do on the job. They drew my attention repeatedly to two major concerns. The first is what Sandra and Celinda raise: How are workplace writers treated by their employers? The interviews reveal some writers taking rhetorical action in response to their own experiences of unfair treatment. The second is about the consequences of their writing for others. Because of this concern, many experienced workplace writers report taking a high degree of responsibility for their on-the-job writing. They sometimes write beyond what their employers require (or desire) as they enact their own standards about what is right. I define this as ethical agency in workplace writing: professionals determine a right course of action that may or may not be prescribed or even permitted by their employers. They nevertheless regard the action as necessary because it either affirms or transcends organizational values. The consequences of their written actions may be beneficial to their employers; more critical for many of these writers, however, are the benefits to other people that result from their ethical agency.

Three sets of mini-cases show professionals writing their way through ethically nuanced situations. The first set picks up where Sandra left me after our classroom discussion, wanting to know more about the conditions under which professionals write handbooks. Three participants report on this from their experiences in the fields of day care, social services, restaurant management, property management, and law. The other two sets examine workers' ethical writing in health care and higher education sectors. Six adult students with job experience at different strata of health care systems identify the ethical interventions they make with everyday genres such as those mandated for documentation, diagnosis, and auditing. Three higher education professionals with experience in instruction, admissions, and human resources exercise ethical agency by working with and against their institutions' norms. I briefly discuss implications of these mini-cases for adult-inclusive higher education.

Handbook Writing across Fields

Handbooks are a common professional genre across employment sectors. Nine out of thirty participants in my study of the writing lives of adult students spoke about writing a handbook, guide, or manual as part of their jobs, although only participants over thirty years of age mentioned this type of writing. That may indicate the degree of experiential authority a writer must embody to produce guiding documents. Procedural writing is taught in some academic settings, yet handbook writers largely learn on the job. Many draw upon models available online or seek samples from peers in similar positions. Creating this common genre is not a neutral matter of simply adapting genre conventions to a particular situation, however. Writers start from scratch or revise an existing handbook in a process that can include researching the genre and the regulatory environment and consulting with supervisors and other colleagues about the goals, substance, and style. Those who discuss procedural writing in depth identify these tasks as necessary, hard, satisfying, enjoyable, and sometimes conflicted. This work poses unique challenges for each writer. Adult student professionals indicate that the act of writing handbooks is laced with rhetorical and ethical considerations that make it among the most difficult writing tasks they do on the job.

Parent Handbook: Authoring under Regulation

Gary Lassiter describes drafting handbooks as "the most daunting experience that I had within writing." Gary is a Black man in his early thirties enrolled in a bachelor of social sciences completer program at NCCU. He is also the lead after-school teacher at his mother's day care whose new administrative duties include writing a handbook. He offers insights about authoring such documents under highly regulated conditions: "If you have a day care, to even start it, you have to have a handbook. And then, you have a parent handbook, of course, for when you enroll. 'Here you go. Here's our packet of what we do, for you to decide if you want to bring your child here, if you don't agree with our philosophy or our mission or how we discipline,' things like that. It's a double whammy. Here's for the state, and here is one for the parent."

Gary explains that while the version for the state is more extensive than the parent handbook, both are subject to guidelines from the Department of Health and Human Services. "I wasn't that familiar with the managerial, administrative working of the day care business until recently. I got to see that . . . there actually is a lot of red tape and a lot of rules and articles and regulations. . . . It doesn't matter if the parent is ever going to read any of this, but you have to put it in there and you have to say it this way. . . . So that was what was daunting about it because I like to just write and just let it flow." Gary's negotiations between his own expressive preferences, his mother's professional values and practices, and state mandates that govern style and content are evident as he tries to ensure that the handbooks accurately translate his mother's priorities into "acceptable professional jargon." He juggles these considerations while learning an unfamiliar genre: "It was complicated for me, just wrapping my mind around the rules and regulations on how to write a handbook." Gary is unusual among participants in that his first attempt at writing a handbook was for a class. He refers to a textbook and samples recommended by his professor, augmenting that by researching other day cares' handbooks and the state's guidelines. "That's how I learn," he says. "I see what other people are doing, and then, I try to take all that and go, 'Okay, well, now, I have to make it my own.'"

Gary's desire to do justice to his mother's perspective and his own sense of authorial ownership suggests that customizing standardized genres for unique situations is an ethical process for workplace writers that involves responsiveness to real people—the parents that a handbook is for, the business owner whose values need to be reflected in it, and the writer who retains some measure of control even in cases where regulatory bodies limit authorial agency.

Internship Handbook: Negotiating Autonomy

Authorial autonomy is also at stake when a project has many minds touching it. Sheri Moss is a Black woman in her early fifties enrolled in NCCU's master of public administration program while working as a staff development trainer for county social services. "We are a fairly new team," she says. "Right now, we're spending a lot of time writing protocols for the agency under the direction of our new leadership. I just completed the internship handbook that we rewrote." The situation she describes speaks to ethical questions about the ways writers are treated on the job, particularly on projects that are subject to oversight.

Sheri respects the workplace hierarchy, as is evident in her approach to drafting: "I don't just sit down and start writing right away. I . . . research first, and I ask questions of how my director may want certain things instead of just stepping out there and writing." With this guidance, she looked forward to having authorial control of rewrites, but she had to negotiate others' different expectations: "With the internship handbook that we just completed . . . my biggest challenge was . . . I was told that this was my baby. This is something I'm going to be working on, and I started working on it. Well, my team lead went behind me . . . she had everything off key. It was off centered and she left some things out. I was discouraged about it. I was really upset about it. . . . . After we had to sit down, and our director went back over it and told her exactly what she wanted, I got that done. . . . I felt satisfied about it after the fact."

Gary's and Sheri's cases both show that authorial control over such projects is important to writers on the job. Sheri's situation in a more hierarchical work environment indicates that when autonomy is promised, then rescinded, it feels like an ethical breach. However, handbooks often represent a collective agreement about policy and practices. They are also rewritten from prior iterations, with histories of authorship that go beyond one person. The process of writing or updating a handbook therefore may become contested as different members of an organization assert their authority to write on behalf of the institution.

Training Guides: Civic Motivations in Corporate Contexts

Jacob Johnson is a white undergraduate psychology major in his mid-thirties who describes procedural guides as enjoyable "little projects" that he has written at several jobs with a goal of "making things understandable." He appreciates the challenge of "trying to hit it exactly on the head" as he guides others. Taking pleasure in this work does not mean it is easy, however: "Going into a lot of these little products, I thought, 'this will be a breeze' and then when I was actually in the heat of it, it proved a little bit more challenging." It is not necessarily the benefit to his employers that motivates Jacob to do this enjoyable but challenging task:

> I am a concierge at an upscale condominium complex. . . . The property management company that hired me took over this complex just prior to me starting, and really with no clue how anything worked. So my job, really, on top of providing just regular day-to-day assistance to the residents of the building, was to really make sense of everything and put together comprehensive guides of procedures. Basically, anything you can think of, I've created a guide to address.
>
> . . . I always knew that I wasn't going to be here long term, necessarily. So I wanted to make sure that there was some sort of system in place for when I left, so that it wouldn't just drop the way it had, right before I started.

Jacob initially describes the guides as employer-driven projects from new business owners who had "no clue how anything worked" before subtly shifting his attention from the employer to the employees. His writing is a preventative act that he hopes will ease the job for future workers, "so it wouldn't just drop the way it had" on him. Jacob's attention to beneficiaries other than his employers is more pronounced as he explains his history with this sort of writing: "I've put together training guides in the last few positions that I worked. At the Social Security disability law firm that I worked at . . . , there was not really a formal training guide. It was sit with somebody for a couple of weeks and hopefully you pick up on everything. I didn't really feel like that was fair to either party, so I worked on putting together a comprehensive training guide."

No one at the law firm directs Jacob to create training guides, although these are presumably beneficial to the firm. Jacob acts on his own beliefs about fair practices. This independent rhetorical act is a subtle way for Jacob to express criticism of standard practices but camouflaged as an unobjectionable "little project." He believes his employers unfairly over rely on job shadowing for their training process; instead of complaining, he assumes responsibility for changing this norm. Whether this writing is assigned or self-initiated, Jacob enacts ethical agency by writing for employees whom he may never know while contributing a sense of order to processes that were in disarray when he first started as a concierge and processes that were previously only conveyed orally at the law firm.

Jacob situates his ability to distill complex information in his experience as a cell phone service salesman, when he also took a principled stand: "I noticed a lot of the other salesmen would say things to customers that would fly right over their head in the sales pitch. . . . I took a much different approach . . . , much to the chagrin of my managers. . . . My approach with . . . customers was really breaking things down in an understandable manner. So that they could really, they had a grasp on everything." Before meeting Jacob, I had not thought of instructional writing as a form of resistance. Yet when he speaks of doing things his way despite chagrined managers, in response to unfair training practices, and as an attempt to bring order to chaotic systems, I perceive Jacob's acts of explanation as ways to rectify undesirable business practices. He offers his knowledge to people—customers and other employees—who are also affected by his employers' actions. His explanatory speaking and instructional writing are not necessarily detrimental to his employers; often they seem beneficial, but he does not appear to be fundamentally motivated by the employers' interests. Jacob's workplace writing is infused instead with a civic ethic.

Writing in Health Care Hierarchies

Health care systems are highly regulated hierarchical work environments in which writing functions within a structured communicative ecology. Procedural action and the writing that accompanies it are central to modern health care operations. The mission of patient and client care undergirds such work, yet that can be obscured by bureaucratic processes of documentation and review that seem shaped by the priorities of insurers, government regulators, and the business side of the mission. These same processes, however, offer means for the professionals in these organizations to exercise ethical agency on behalf of clients and patients. The adult students who spoke with me about their writing in health care settings indicate that standardized modes of professional communication can be part of a patient-oriented work ethic. For instance, as Atul Gawande discusses in *The Checklist Manifesto,* well-designed forms and procedural checklists reduce error in complex medical processes that have life-and-death consequences. Small errors in codes may interfere with patients' access to care and coverage; therefore, even data entry is part of the ethical imperative of health professions. Documenting interactions with patients, auditing standard processes, training providers, and redesigning software can all be conceived as ethical acts when their aim is to improve outcomes for patients or clients. Health care professionals regularly negotiate competing priorities when centering their care for individuals within larger structures.

I examine ethical dimensions of the writing that health care professionals perform through the experiences of six working adult students, four in master's programs (public administration, pharmacology, and mental health counseling), one undergraduate, and a law student. Their health care system jobs include office support, multiple direct care positions, and medical compliance, collectively representing the possibilities for agency within several strata of health care hierarchies.

Meticulous Recordkeeping, Minimal Autonomy

The ethical dimensions of medical documentation may not be legible at first glance. Especially in positions of low autonomy, ethical agency can be obscured. Kimberly Robinson is a Black student in her mid-thirties enrolled in NCCU's master of public administration program. She discusses a past clerical job in a medical office, providing an example of low-autonomy writing in which automated systems shape and provide content: "They have so many different softwares now that they're built to the needs of the business, in health care. From what my line of service was . . . for the most part, it was already built into a database for you to do, like calendars. Everything was just already set up. You just go in and fill in the information, send it out. As far as the preop information, that's already hospital system generated. So, it's not really anything that you have to do." Kimberly's phrases, "fill in the information" and "system generated," indicate limited agency for writers performing routine clerical duties in health care settings. However, inaccuracies at this point could have consequences for Kimberly's colleagues, their patients, and the overall system.

The writing performed by a certified nursing assistant (CNA) in both urgent care and home health care settings is less automated than Kimberly's databases, although it is driven by routine documentation protocols. Paula Thacker is a working Black student in her mid-thirties enrolled in the university's undergraduate completer degree program in social sciences. She explains the ubiquity of a CNA's documentation responsibilities: "You have to document everything. It's a lot of writing, just documenting that patient's day. How many meals they ate, if they're on a liquid diet, solids, what types of food they're able to eat. I've had to write down insurance information, . . . assisting the patients with writing their name, address, and a description of the injury that they've had." The point of this meticulous writing is communication to other members of the care team. "We have to document what you've done basically, like if the patient had any issues or concerns to report to the nurse, so . . . whoever's coming in for the next shift . . . they'll know what's happened and what's going on." Continuity of care depends upon interactions between patients and clinicians and between members of a care team. The thorough writing that Paula describes augments these in-person exchanges with a record of observations, actions, and discussions oriented toward providing responsive patient care across multiple shift rotations and changing personnel.

Clinicians' Dilemmas

Documentation for continuity of care is also a major activity reported by three clinicians who have broader responsibilities than CNAs. They all negotiate between direct patient care and their responsibilities for maintaining the written record of that care. Missy[2] is a Nigerian primary care physician with five years of clinical experience who enrolled in NCCU's master of pharmacology program in her mid-thirties. She relies on notes and memory to document patient histories, examination findings, and diagnoses. She develops plans of care from these notes. Her description of the process shows the difficulty of balancing attention to the patient with the demands of documentation:

M You have to take a lot of history from patients. You cannot forget anything, so you have to write it down. You have to listen, but the same time, try to jot down the important points of what the person is saying, and then later develop it into a proper note. . . . . Then you examine the patient. You have to write down your examination findings, and then your own notes, so what you think the diagnosis is, you have to write that down. You have to write your plan of care.

C What's the hardest thing about that kind of writing?

M You just have to make sure you don't forget any detail. Once the patient has told you, you must put it down. . . . It's about remembering, because when the patient is talking to you, you can't be writing everything, or you can't record. . . . You just have to remember or have a way of writing it that you won't distract yourself or distract the person you're talking to.

Missy's account suggests competing ethical frameworks that drive medical professionals' actions. One is the imperative to attend to the patient directly. The other is to document the interaction so it can be used for diagnostics, care plans, and billing. These are both nonnegotiable responsibilities of the job, but attempting to simultaneously attend to a person and attend to writing compromises the physician's attention. There are situations in which patients' needs are so urgent that writing must be deferred: "I used to work in the emergency department. There are times that you just have to attend to the patient and leave notes for later. . . . . You can't say, 'Oh I have to write down what this patient told me,' and then you leave it. Patients die. . . . There's the time for action where you just have to attend first, and then when the patient is stable, you get back to your notes. . . . Then in between, something can happen. You have to stop [writing]. Go again to attend to the patient, come back to finish your notes." Missy's normal professional writing practice is thus sometimes covert and often interrupted as she toggles between providing care and writing it up.

Clinical writing in an emergency department offers an extreme example of this tension between competing ethical and temporal demands on physicians, but other clinicians face dilemmas too as they decide what and how much to write about their clients and in what formats. Two white counseling interns, one with no prior therapeutic experience and one with years in clinical settings, have different perspectives on this. An experienced counselor in her fifties, Micheale Collie notes that some practices are about developing long-term therapeutic relationships. Yet even when the job entails a shorter time frame of "just trying to get someone clean, stable, and out to the next level of care," counselors translate clients' extremely personal stories into information that can be used to diagnose, justify treatment, and provide referrals. She says, "I feel privileged to be able to sit with this person and have them share their story with me." Akin to Missy's perspective as an attending physician, Micheale's attentiveness to the client occurs side by side with her responsibility to write up what she learns so the client can obtain further care: "They're having to be vulnerable and share all of this with a stranger. . . . I can appreciate the position they're in and they're basically having to . . . bare their souls . . . in order for me to get this information."

One major challenge for newer practitioners is determining how much to document from clinical sessions. Micheale's less experienced classmate, Stephanie Levin, is a career-changer in her mid-forties interning at the university counseling center as part of NCCU's master's program in mental health counseling. She grapples with the unfamiliar documentation requirements of her role. Although she taught English and has an MFA in creative writing, she regards client notes as "a very frustrating type of writing": "When I started out, I was writing narratives. This is what happened and then this, and then the therapist thought this and then the client said that. I was writing a story. And of course that's not sustainable, nor is it relevant. But I was so afraid I would forget when I saw the client again, forget what we had talked about. And I don't ever want to look blankly at someone. . . . So I did that. But . . . it was unsustainable and it's shortened over time . . . And now . . . it's as brief as I can be." While Paula, the CNA, documented for other members of a care team,

Stephanie's primary audience is her future self; thus she tries to write thoroughly enough to feel prepared for future sessions. Her statement "I don't ever want to look blankly at someone" also reflects other-directed ethics, an awareness of what a therapist's blank look might feel like to a client. As she becomes more at ease with professional practice, brief notes suffice for picking up where she and a client left off. Stephanie learned the terse style not from coursework but instead from her supervisor, who provided examples and feedback until she "got to a comfortable place where I felt like I could do it."

The more experienced clinician, Micheale, distinguishes between private notes that are for her own reference and those that could go into circulation, a distinction with consequences for clients and the therapeutic relationship. Micheale worked fourteen years as a counselor, but her certifications lapsed during a long illness. Once recovered, she restarted NCCU's master's program, which required working full-time as an unpaid intern in a detox unit. She draws on that and her prior counseling experience when discussing writing in this profession. Micheale writes assessment notes, discharge summaries, treatment plans, and progress notes, all of which are part of the medical record that is available to other clinicians, clients, and insurers. Micheale explains why the concise style that is so challenging for Stephanie is important for clinicians: "Progress notes . . . that go into the medical records, you don't put all the details of what's going on in a person's life, because you don't want a clinical judgment to possibly be revealed to a client through their medical records, because they can have access to their records." Micheale learned the hard way that her writings in the medical record may be subpoenaed by the courts, which can have unintended consequences: "I've been subpoenaed before with a child protective services case. . . . I had to appear as a witness, and read from the medical record with my client sitting three feet from me. . . . That was a real quick lesson in, yeah, I don't want to put too much personal information in this chart."

Micheale since learned to write some observations privately, outside of the formal medical record. "If I have concerns, I'm going to keep those in a process note, because that was a horrible experience." She defines process notes as writing that counselors "keep for themselves about the people they're working with, which are actually more individualized and get into much more of the meat of what's happening with the client" than the progress notes that are part of the record. She regards separating them from the official record as a critical strategy for protecting clients and therapeutic relationships:

> Those notes cannot be subpoenaed by the court or anyone else, because to the rest of the world nobody knows they exist. Being able to write process notes that I keep locked in a safe place I only have access to, helps me . . . make sure that I'm meeting the clients' needs, and also helps me keep a running commentary on what I think is going on, or what I think would be helpful for

> the client. I like being able to keep that separate from what's going in the medical record that will become a part of that person's history that people could subpoena, and those notes could end up being read by judges or attorneys or God forbid in the court in front of the client. . . . it can destroy a clinical relationship faster than anything else.

Micheale's private notes about her clients are a form of client-centered ethical agency. Keeping some writing out of circulation is a strategy that requires professional discernment, as does enactment of Micheale's diagnostic philosophy, which at times is at odds with the business side of clinical practice: "I don't always agree with the fact that we have to diagnose everybody who comes through the door . . . so that we can get paid. . . . It's when you get into the more serious diagnoses, like if you think there is a personality disorder, or if the person has an eating disorder, or if the person has a psychotic disorder of some kind like schizophrenia. Those diagnoses will follow the client for the rest of their lives." Micheale navigates the line between insurer-driven business practices and her ethical determination to protect clients from the permanency of diagnostic records: "I have struggled with systems and coworkers who were like, 'this person definitely has this,' and if I don't agree with that, then we have to take it up a notch and negotiate with a supervisor. I'm not quick to judge, I'm not quick to label somebody with something that I'm not convinced they have because I don't want them to be stuck with that label if it's not accurate." One facet of ethical agency in professional writing is thus restraint, either by choosing not to write something such as a diagnosis or choosing not to place certain observations into the formal medical record.

Direct care providers Paula, Missy, Stephanie, and Micheale all use writing as members of care teams whose priorities center on individual patients and clients. Their writing helps those they serve receive continuity of care and appropriate treatment. Direct care professionals work within a legal system in which medical records are subject to subpoenas as evidence. They also work in a corporate and regulatory system in which providers' notes function not just as information for a care team but also as coded documentation of billable activity that is subject to review by multiple entities beyond other caregivers. It is this wider rhetorical, ethical, judicial, economic, and regulatory ecosystem that Micheale and others like her must navigate as they deliberate what to write and what to withhold from clients' medical records.

Principled Auditing

The medical records painstakingly created by clerical and clinical professionals are subject to review as systems manage risks, reduce inefficiencies, and improve patient care. First-year law student Kenton Spencer is an Asian American in his early fifties who is a health care systems compliance analyst. His job demands broad analytical, rhetorical, and ethical capacities analogous to the legal profession he studies, although each field requires its own subject area expertise. Kenton's principled stance on health care and his understanding of where his work fits into the institutional system enable him to perform audits with keen attention to the effects on multiple stakeholders in that system, including administrators, clinicians, and patients. Auditing is a rhetorically intricate process that entails analyzing medical documentation, comparing billing and workflow data, drafting findings, listening to practitioners, making recommendations, and training others to enact those recommendations. His audit reports typically circulate to clinicians, information technologists, and operational leadership. Although all these audiences matter, Kenton prioritizes clinicians because they are often the ones tasked with improvement. For a compliance officer to be perceived as a supporter by those who are subject to audit is an uphill rhetorical job. Kenton explains clinicians' ambivalence and how he attempts to shift the perception of auditing from adversarial to collaborative by articulating a shared ethic of taking care of patients:

> When you hear compliance, it's just like talking to a dentist or IRS, it's just not something you really look forward to. Right? . . . I mean you don't wake up and go, "God, I hope I hear from compliance. I just really just want to see what more paperwork I got to do today." . . . .
>
> I remove that cringe. . . . When I interact with people, the first thing I do is I thank them for their service, which is true. . . . Especially now . . . , these are people that are literally putting their lives on the line to try to take care of people.[3] And I tell them, "I'm here to support you. . . . . But the only way I can support you is for us to have an open, honest dialogue as to your challenges."

The fact that Kenton's wife is a physician may influence his ability to empathize with clinicians' ambivalence. He knows their central focus, like Missy's, is their patients. Kenton explains that his approach is to position himself as serving those being audited and their patients. His verbs, "support," "help," "provide," "work for," "assist," and "advocate," convey that stance. "I'm here to help. . . . I'm here to provide a service to the clinician staff because in the end the real end users or stakeholders are the patients. . . . So that's my approach. My . . . two key stakeholders that I work for are the physicians and clinicians or nurses and the patients. . . . My role is to assist them. . . . I take a process approach. I don't sit there and go, 'You did this because you suck.' I am like, okay, 'Where are we failing you?' And to help in delivering the services. And which way are we creating unnecessary risks to the patient." Kenton expects providers to perceive auditors as shame agents, so he repositions himself as an advocate using the audit process to reveal the system's failures, not the clinicians'. In his efforts to build trust with those who are subject to an audit, Kenton is not only deflating unpalatable perceptions about compliance officers, he also is resisting common hierarchical blaming structures. "It's not blame the doctors . . . , blame the staff and the clinics, and then go on your way. . . . That's not my approach. . . . I think most people have the best intentions. . . . You've got to give people the benefit of doubt, especially when you work in systems." Positioning himself as an ally to providers is a crucial rhetorical move that enables Kenton to gather data under the premises of a shared ethic of professional care that reflects their joint commitment to patients. "Once we have that honest, critical conversation, then it's like it opens up."

Kenton's regard for the humanity of people who work in and are served by health care systems permeates his writing responsibilities. With his background in finance,[4] Kenton might logically take a fiscal bottom line approach to compliance. That aspect of auditing matters to him, but his motivating principle is quality patient care. This is apparent when I ask: "If you were training a new compliance analyst to write this kind of report, what would be the most important thing that they should know?" Kenton focuses on quality. He regards training an auditor to develop reports from myriad data points as ethically analogous to training providers to document their observations and decisions:

> . . . Your work has to be of the highest quality so it can be understandable. It's no different than when we train new providers in our compliance training [on] the importance of documentation. It's not just because we're into paperwork. It's because it's patient care. And I always say, "Look, you want to be able to communicate the information to another team member, to another provider who may follow up if your patient goes to a hospital or if they have to go to a specialist. Because in the end the best thing to think about is how would you want someone you love and care for to be treated? And if you don't think your work is up to snuff for someone you love, then it's not up to snuff for your patients." So it's the same . . . thing for someone I'm training [to audit]. . . . "Is the kind of work this is truly representative of you . . . ? And if it [isn't], then rethink it."

Kenton introduces three ethical principles in this discussion of training: (1) Treat patients as carefully as you would loved ones. (2) Pay attention to the useability of your work for others in the system. (3) Your work quality represents you.

He elaborates on what constitutes quality, usable audit reports: "Make sure that your findings are sound, logically. You know, that the numbers match. That your calculations match. And then think about your recommendations. Are they actionable? Are they too vague? . . . Are they something that someone can sit and be like, 'Okay, I can actually use this to improve,' versus just a wasted sentence, like 'We'll conduct a further review in this period,' or something that's just nonspecific, that's fluff. That's just like laziness. . . . You need to find a recommendation that's going to make things better and that you can stand on." Kenton's intensity about the writer's responsibility is tempered by his final advice to auditor trainees: "Your supervisors are going to touch it, leadership's going to touch it, other people are going to touch it." He therefore advocates for professional humility; individual work is part of a system: "Don't take any constructive criticism personally. . . . Don't own this too much. . . . once you finish it, it belongs to the system. It's not yours. . . . you learn to let it go. Once you're done, it's a reflection of you. Absolutely. You know, most things are in some way. But on the other hand, we got to learn to let it go. Because . . . the system owns it." Kenton's on-the-job development of situated ethical agency within a large system models how rhetorical and ethical knowledge accrue density with increased professional experience. This degree of immersive, sustained, on-the-job learning cannot be replicated, but it could be leveraged in higher education.

The Writing of Higher Education Professionals

Like workers in health care systems, higher education professionals work within hierarchies that place limitations on the scope of their agency. Nevertheless, three adults seeking advanced degrees at NCCU discuss cases in which they exercise their own values within such systems, sometimes in violation of system rules and norms, and sometimes as a way to hold institutions accountable to their stated principles. These men speak from their professional experience in instructional, admissions, and human resources roles to reveal what it is like to take a stance within these systems and how their writing functions as principled action. Their stories reveal a kind of moral elasticity in the relationships between institutions and their employees. As with the handbook examples, the ethical acts of writing that these academic employees take may or may not directly benefit their employers, but they perform them out of their own moral codes about how to treat other people. These codes transcend institutional culture.

Subverting the Canned Curriculum

De'Von Carter is a Black law student in his mid-thirties whose educational history is the most accelerated of any other cases in this book; his professional advancement has been equally rapid.[5] He enrolled full-time at a state university directly after high school where he earned a bachelor's degree in electronics computer networking within four years. De'Von's career progression includes a series of rapid promotions in information technology and analytics positions in defense, banking, and other corporate settings. While working full-time, he completed a master's degree in information systems security at a private for-profit university only two years after finishing his bachelor's degree. De'Von works as an information technology solutions architect and vice president of a bank while raising a family, running his own cybersecurity consulting firm, and serving as the conference director for a regional information security organization. He is also in his third year of the part-time evening law program at NCCU.

While rising in his own career, De'Von sought opportunities to mentor others interested in advancement in information technology and security fields. "I always wanted to teach at the college level," he said, so he began as an adjunct instructor at ITT Technical Institute, where he taught for five years. ITT Tech was a notorious private for-profit that closed in 2016 after the U.S. Department of Education ceased to guarantee loans for its students. Although he characterizes his other positions as requiring more intensive and advanced professional writing, De'Von's discussion of this job plainly reveals how writing functions as an act of ethical agency within corporate structures:

> I didn't know anything about ITT Tech's business model when I first started. I just thought . . . , "Oh, it's a tech school. They probably pay less money to get a degree, and I'm going to be helping people. Yay." And then I find out from one of my students they're paying twenty-five grand a year. And I'm like, "Wait. What? You're paying how much?" It made me want to teach them better. It made me want to work harder for them. Because it's like, "These kids are going to get out of here, if they do this for four years, that's one hundred grand in debt. And they have a degree from ITT Tech?" . . . It made me work harder to make sure I tried to give them the best opportunity I could.

De'Von's realizations about the mismatch between what students were paying and what their credentials would mean for them was one motivator for changing his teaching. The other was outdated curriculum. Development of curriculum and course materials was outside the parameters of his adjunct job description, but he acted on what he saw as an ethical imperative:

> In those jobs, the PowerPoints were supposed to be provided, because they're adjunct positions. They're supposed to provide the materials in those particular teaching gigs. And so, they're not . . . like at the university, where you find your textbook and you have to develop curriculum. . . . There [ITT Tech], the curriculum is already developed. You walk in, they hand you a book, they hand you a thumb drive with slides on it, and they say, "Go." And the problem with that is that most of their stuff was incorrect or outdated, or it just didn't apply anymore.
>
> So what ended up happening is, most of the adjunct instructors there would end up having to basically fix PowerPoints or just build new ones. We had to do a lot of that. . . . . They weren't making us do it, it just needed to be done.

De'Von subverts the authorized curriculum because it contradicts his professional experience and students would otherwise be paying a premium for outdated content. His moral obligation to his students exceeds his contractual obligations to the employer. De'Von and his fellow adjunct instructors demonstrate agency by determining independently that the prescribed curriculum fails their own professional standards for ethical teaching. They then author new material regardless of their employer's denial of authorial roles for instructors on adjunct appointments.

This ethical act simultaneously works for and against the institution. Although unauthorized, corrections to the course content improve the value of the institution's credentials. Given the comparisons of enrollments by institutional types that I document in chapter 1, many of the students De'Von taught are probably Black working-class adult students who enrolled on the promise that the credentials would improve their professional prospects. De'Von could not guarantee that, but he could ensure that what he taught was current, and he could advise students of other options. For the latter, he let students know about community college programs that charged a fraction of ITT Tech's tuition. He told his introductory students: "Look, here's the deal. You got three weeks in this class to figure out whether you like it or not. If within that three weeks you figure out that you don't like it and you don't want to be here, then you need to get out of this school immediately before you're locked into that tuition." De'Von disregards the interests of the institution because his ethical responsibilities as a mentor supersede his responsibilities to an employer, especially one that casts him in a subordinate role as an adjunct employee. Advising his students honestly is the right thing to do.

Other adult students who work in higher education reveal that these kinds of decisions are not confined to employees at for-profit institutions. Writing—and other rhetorical acts—can be forms of situated ethical agency that resist codification as merely operating for or against the interests of an institution, or the employee, or the people the institution serves. The subsequent cases show further nuance as an admissions counselor and a human resources professional work through their systems' protocols with keen attention to the ethical treatment of prospective students and their families and prospective university employees.

Humanizing Templates in Admissions

David[6] is a Black man in his late forties who left a fourteen-year career in undergraduate admissions to attend NCCU's master's program in school counseling. David's discussion about professional correspondence demonstrates his ethical approaches for acting as an agent of the institution while treating prospective students and their families with care reflective of his personal values.

Email is a large part of admissions writing. David describes using templates and shortcut keys for efficiency: "Having those types of tools and templates . . . allows me to focus on the content, the feeling that I'm trying to convey," he says. He adopts a personalized approach to correspondence that is scaffolded by those shortcuts. His most important emails are "assuring parents and students of a holistic comprehensive review of their application." This assurance must be worded carefully to protect his employer from legal action. "To be very frank," he says, "the university . . . [has] been sued for its practice of affirmative action." He explains that the writings he does in admissions are subject to legal discovery: "Discoverability traditionally is not something recorded or videoed, it's what you have written, what you summarize." To minimize legal risk when conveying admissions decisions requires "being a very judicious, thoughtful writer." David explains that in this context, "less is more." He corresponds with prospective students with an awareness that what he writes might not remain just between them. The legal landscape means this writing has to be considered quasi-public, "as if you were going to see it published on the front page."

In a legal climate that necessitates such self-consciousness, it would be understandable for admissions personnel to stick to templates that have been vetted by university lawyers. However, David embodies a caring philosophy about his interactions with prospective students and their families. He keeps the legal considerations in mind, but he prioritizes writing in ways that address the feelings of those receiving his messages and that reflect his professional ethos. "You want to convey authority, you want to convey gentleness, you want to convey that you're knowledgeable. . . . There's always . . . a pressure to make sure you're conveying something in writing that doesn't make somebody feel less than or hostile to you while still conveying warmth and empathy and understanding." The university's acceptance rate of about 20 percent meant that David was frequently responsible for delivering bad news: "I wrote a lot of emails to disappointed students. . . . 'I hate giving this tough information to you, you have some options, but I can't help you with your current requests to have a space in this first year class.' . . . I found that high stress . . . right up until the last days with my job because I don't want to treat somebody transactionally like a number, that's just not what a person should do."

David negotiates the ethical, emotional, and legal landscape of professional writing in university admissions by infusing templated correspondence with his personal touch, "trying to be myself," while fulfilling an institutional role.

Redressing Lapses in Human Resources

Christopher Genwright is a Black veteran in his early forties who works full-time while enrolled in NCCU's master of public administration program. His associate's and bachelor's degrees, paralegal certificate, and graduate coursework are the result of enrollment in six different institutions, mostly public, that he attended while employed. Directly from high school, he enlisted in the U.S. Air Force, where he served for five years, attending community college simultaneously until he completed an associate's degree. While stationed in Japan, he took further classes at a branch campus of a U.S. state university, then he completed his sociology degree at a third public institution after leaving the service. Veterans benefits and loans made completing his undergraduate degrees feasible. Much of his professional experience after the military has been in human resource departments in the corporate sector and at three different universities; tuition benefits from these employers have enabled him to pursue graduate studies while working.

At the time of our interview, Christopher had recently drafted two email templates to address a long-standing loose end in the human resource department's career fair practices. He explains that career fair attendees add their contact information to a sign-up sheet; it bothers him that his group historically did nothing with that information. "Whenever we go to a career fair, we have sign-in sheets at our booths. People were just signing in for years and there was no communication going out to them.... Whenever they were signing it, they're like, 'Are we going to be on the mailing list or something?' And we're like, 'I don't know.'" It strikes him as an ethical lapse that career fair attendees expect signing up to result in some response, yet the department had no process for doing so. Attendees "put their name on these sheets that we just stick in books and never look at again." Christopher addresses that lapse: "I... came up with an email... that welcomed them to our website. If they're looking for jobs, how they can sign up for interest calls. It was basically like a system generated email whenever you sign up or whenever you check what areas that you're interested in, and it just sent them an email with a link to the jobs where they can read it and apply for it if they want to, all these things that we can just copy and paste on an email to these people that come to the career fairs."

Christopher made separate email templates for the general public and for veterans that reflect differences in hiring regulations. "When we go to veteran's career fairs, we like to add a special bit in there about veterans receiving... preference for state employment." His use of the collective pronoun indicates that he speaks for human resources as a whole in their recruitment approaches for veteran applicants, yet his own identity as a veteran likely amplifies his awareness of the relevant regulations and his sense of duty to create customized correspondence templates for this group.

University employees with ideas for improvements often cannot simply enact changes independently. Christopher tells me, "I did those two... email templates today, and now I'm just trying to work them through and get them approved, so next time we go to a career fair we can start using them and actually using those sign-in sheets for something instead of collecting dust." This effort exemplifies the possibilities for a professional to exert ethical agency on behalf of both an employer and the broader public within the constraints of bureaucratic processes. Nobody asks Christopher to draft the templates. He sees a problem, and he takes the initiative. The chain of command he mentions is a common condition of authorship in large, hierarchical institutions: even something as seemingly straightforward as creating boilerplate for corresponding with potential job applicants must go through an approval process, which entails more email, more negotiation. It is a system in which employees can initiate ethical improvements but are expected to seek authorization.

Just as David is aware of the laws affecting undergraduate admissions, Christopher is attentive to the legal landscape of human resources. He refers to this professional knowledge in his public administration classes during discussions about equal opportunity employment practices: "It's always good to have an insight, an HR insight, especially, to discuss in class. With me working in employment and staffing for so many years, and also in equal opportunity, . . . I have a great perspective on some of the things that we do, especially if a position is underrepresented, because a lot of people, if you're on the outside looking in, you're just looking at, 'This job was posted, this office is all white and they just continually hire white people.' But then somebody like me, I'm like, 'Well, actually, nobody but white people applied for this job.'"

In a reversal from the usual positioning of adult students as outsiders in academia, Christopher perceives his less experienced classmates as outsiders peering into professional practice. They question it but do not yet understand it. Christopher sees the value of his insider status as an experienced professional who has handled equal opportunity issues in hiring because he can provide real scenarios relevant to the course concepts. In these classrooms, he also shares his strategies for advocating for equitable practices. For example, he describes researching a job candidate pool and emailing a hiring department to call attention to qualified candidates from underrepresented populations who would otherwise have been overlooked: "I would . . . look at the pool and see who's a woman or a minority, and then if they're qualified or as qualified as some of the other candidates, I'm sending an email to the department like, 'Hey, there's a few people in the pool. This position is underrepresented. Would you like to take a second look at these applicants and see if you want to bring them in for an interview just to give them a shot at the position?'" In describing such firm, principled, and tactful rhetorical actions in his graduate courses, Christopher demonstrates the ethical agency that experienced professionals can exert even in highly regulated environments. Combining his awareness of the law with his own principles, he sees it as his job not only to ensure compliance with employment law but also to hold his employer to its professed standards. Furthermore, in both of the writing scenarios that Christopher describes—the job fair follow-up templates and his correspondence with hiring departments—the workaday genre of email is revealed as a tool in efforts at achieving equity within organizations. Christopher's examples show that during the crafting of such mundane documents, workers can strategically act on behalf of their employers while animating the ethical principles they espouse.

The extent to which any institution can be said to be an ethical enterprise is only a result of the actions of the people who comprise that institution. At these sites of practice, writing is a critical vehicle for ethical action whether that affects one person, such as a diagnostic decision, or many, like a recruitment template. The writers in this chapter show that acts of ethical agency in professional contexts occur on a spectrum from alignment to conflict in relation to the prevailing practices of the institutions they work for. Their ethical acts may be amplifications of institutionally held principles, such as the audits Kenton conducts in alignment with a health care system's core mission of patient care. On the other end of the spectrum, they may be subversive practices that reduce harm caused by the institution, such as De'Von ensuring his students are aware of affordable educational options. Jacob's training guide, written in response to his own experiences of poor orientation to a job, occupies the nebulous zone between an institutionally endorsed and a subversive practice. What many of these writers share is a desire to assert agency when they notice lapses. As Kenton says, "You need to find a recommendation that's going to make things better and that you can stand on." This statement asserts the professional's ethical obligation to be an agent for improvement. By this measure, Sheri's self-advocacy when her supervisor overrode the autonomy she had been promised on a handbook project is as much an act of ethical agency as Christopher's correspondence with hiring committees to ensure they pay attention to all qualified candidates in an applicant pool. To be successful in these actions requires that these writers hew to their own principles and express them with awareness of workplace genres and the systems, hierarchies, institutional interests, and legal and cultural contexts within which they write. Holding institutions accountable requires negotiating power relationships with sensitivity, especially in hierarchical organizations where writers must often work through a chain of command to advocate for principled change.

Several participants mention points of contact between their professional experience and their academic studies that suggest implications for pedagogy, curriculum, and the career preparatory discourse that fuels much educational practice. For relative novices among these adult students, the school-to-work paradigm retains some validity. For instance, Gary points to undergraduate coursework as his introduction to how to write handbooks; this affords him practice with the genre in a fictional situation before attempting to write a handbook for his mother's day care business. He is able to build on this orientation to basic genre conventions to face the greater challenge of negotiating the regulatory environment, his mothers' specifications, and his own desires to make the work his own. The case of Stephanie, who was changing careers, also affirms the college-to-career direction of academic learning to professional application, although she indicates that she did not learn about writing clinical notes during her counseling classes. It is her internship supervisor who provides that guidance. Her graduate program's inclusion of experiential learning as part of the curriculum demonstrates institutional acknowledgement that classes alone are not sufficient for teaching the lived complexity of professional practice.

However, the school-to-work paradigm fails to account for workforce knowledge of more experienced professionals. This can cause ethical lapses in approaches that are based on teaching only novices. For instance, Micheale's counseling internship seems like a step back to her on two counts. First, she is paying the university to learn to apply counseling theory in a real-world setting, but she already has over a decade of experience doing so. She also mentions that the critical distinction she makes between private process notes and on-the-record progress notes is impossible to enact at her internship site because interns have nowhere to lock away their notes about clinical interactions. Her professional knowledge thus exceeds the options for practice that are available to her in this school-sponsored experiential setting. Micheale's case points to ethical issues regarding programs that mandate field work on the assumption that students lack professional experience.

Even in a program designed for working adults, Kenton finds a mismatch between his knowledge of professional practice and the writing he is expected to produce as a first-year law student. Compared to his fluency in professional writing within complex health care systems, he finds the assigned legal briefs difficult to write because they seem to him to be formulaic, oversimplified academic genres that are radically decontextualized from actual practice. It is impossible for him to apply his nuanced understanding of how writing works in professional life to these assignments that require a much narrower interpretation of the rhetorical situation.

Christopher's case offers one glimpse of adult-inclusive education in which classroom culture enables academic and professional lives to function as mutually informing sites of learning. He mentions no friction when he brings his human resources experience to bear on class discussions in the master of public administration program, indicating that his experiential knowledge is welcome. He provides living cases of ethical agency fresh from the workplace as opportunities for himself and his classmates to examine course concepts in relation to his concurrent professional experience.

I have occasionally heard graduate teaching assistants and new faculty express trepidation about yielding the floor to adult learners like those who inform this chapter. Such instructors may be reluctant to share authority that they have only newly established themselves. Yet doing so can be beneficial in mixed-age learning environments. Sharing authority lets adult students know that their experiential knowledge is valued for the ways it complements and complicates academic learning. Even—especially—when what adult students know contradicts what is being taught, as Sandra's knowledge did in my technical writing class, those can be critical moments for instructional openness because unpacking such conflict has the capacity to deepen learning for everyone who shares the educational space.

5

Writing with Emotion

I did not plan to study emotion. I set out to learn about the breadth of writing that adult students do across their life experiences, why it matters to them, and what resources they draw upon to do their writing. Yet, repeatedly, participants alerted me to emotion's relevance to writing across all areas of their lives. What they teach me about writing with emotion eclipses what I understood from years of study and classroom interactions because academic culture—including in the field of rhetoric and composition—still predominantly segregates reason from emotion. Although some scholars note the uptake of theories of affect and emotion within rhetoric and composition (Edbauer Rice 2008; Jiang 2024; Micciche 2016), my initial research goals were consistent with the field's mainstream, which largely has relegated emotion to creative, expressive, and literary genres presumably outside of the discipline's purview. Emotion has been present, of course, in my research and teaching. When working with writers and writing, how could it not be? But I tacitly bracketed emotion until the spotlight of adult students' attention to it became too bright to ignore. The students in this chapter show that, in myriad ways, emotion is highly consequential to their writing.

In the cases examined in chapters 3 and 4, the traces of emotion are already evident. Tamara Vanie's choreography to "Lovely Day" emerges from sadness. She journals her way through a difficult pregnancy. The speech she writes invokes "hurt" and "sacrifice," and she delivers it despite feeling "terrified of public speaking." Writing on the job is also suffused with emotion. Sheri Moss feels "discouraged" and "upset" while drafting a handbook. Gary Lassiter feels "daunted." Emotion furthermore factors into how professionals think of their readers. David wants to convey "gentleness," "warmth," and "empathy" in his admissions letters. Kenton Spencer seeks to defray clinicians' dread of being audited, and he calls on their empathy for patients. The impetus for workplace writers' ethical agency is often sparked by emotion; writers like Jacob Johnson and De'Von Carter must feel that something is wrong before they do something about it.

In this chapter, I work through other situations shared by adult undergraduates to theorize emotion's relationship to writing. Although students speak with me about emotion's relevance to a wide range of writing that they do, including on the job and for coursework, this chapter focuses on self-initiated writing rather than writing required by others. Like adult undergraduates themselves, this kind of writing is less studied than academic and workplace writing. These cases therefore are opportunities to examine writers' emotional agency independent from assigned situations. The quoted undergraduates major in interdisciplinary social sciences, English, nursing, art, and psychology. They are in their thirties through early fifties, and the majority are Black women. Paula Thacker, Lisa Fakir, and Gary Lassiter discuss writing as a transformative means for enduring difficult emotions, for expressing emotion, and for leveraging emotions strategically to redress harms in many areas of their lives. Several interrelated situations raised by Adrienne Long provide the grounds for broader conceptual development about writing with emotion. The writing she does to advocate for herself and other adult students is saturated with emotional energy.

To these writers' cases, I apply scholarship from diverse fields to conceptualize emotion, emotional agency, and their relationship to writing and rhetoric. This analysis reveals that by using writing to express and to move through emotion, and by using emotion to catalyze change, writers can assert emotional agency in situations that otherwise feel out of their control. Their cases show writing's capacity as an embodied practice of critical emotional agency that utilizes individual and social dimensions of emotion to alter the self and influence environments, including facilitating institutional change.

Collins situates emotion within Black feminist epistemologies rooted in African humanism. In this tradition, individual uniqueness of expression matters, an ethic of care enables empathy across difference, and the presence of emotion validates rather than detracts from argument, with reason and emotion functioning dialogically (2000). Collins asserts that emotion signifies the importance of an issue, and it forges connections. hooks also rejects segregation of emotion from intellectual practice, noting that "emotions keep us aware or alert" (1994, 155). Micciche calls for researchers of writing to reinterpret emotion as something we do rather than something that we have. She argues that we should use "emotion as a category of analysis" (2007, 108) because it is integral to humans' embodied "efforts to reason, communicate, and act meaningfully" (4). In alignment with this idea of emotion as an action, scholars in several fields use the term "emotional agency," but in ways that reflect disciplinary differences about the locus of agency. Theories based in psychology emphasize the individual, whereas other fields position emotion as a social phenomenon that is best understood in circulation. Organizational psychologists offer an example of the former in their model for how emotional agency functions for individuals in work environments (Hökkä et al. 2022). Communication scholars and sociologists, however, position emotional agency within social change theory (Krone and Dougherty 2015; Weenink and Spaargaren 2016). Both ways of thinking about emotional agency are evident in how adult students talk about writing with emotion.

Hökkä and colleagues (2022) theorize that emotional agency can be regarded first as a personal attribute, meaning having the competence to recognize the emotions of oneself and others and to be able to express them. A key part of this team's model of emotional agency is individuals having a sufficiently granular vocabulary to express their own feelings and to read the room for others' emotions. These researchers define emotional agency further as behavior or action by which individuals change emotions in self and others, thus having influence within the emotional climate of groups and institutions. In other words, a psychological model of agency focuses on ways individuals use their competence at understanding emotions to move themselves and others from one state of emotion to another. This relational emotional movement goes beyond one-on-one interpersonal interactions to potentially have large group effects.

Writing figures into this version of emotional agency through theories of reflection, although when compositionists discuss writing as a mode of reflection, it is generally for intellectual rather than emotional purposes. Recent work that examines emotion in students' reflective writing points to the normalcy of this separation: "Conventional metacognitive approaches that focus on critical awareness often bypass the significant component of *feeling* and the insights reflection can yield regarding students' emotional relationship to writing" (Miller et al. 2023, 486). Although emotional aspects of reflective activity have long been downplayed, Yancey indicates that multiple modes interact during such practices. She writes: "When we reflect, we call upon the cognitive, the affective, the intuitive, putting these into play with each other" (Yancey 1998, 6). Yancey also discusses reflection as a means of transforming experience and "a knowledge-making activity keyed to uncertainty and ambiguity" (2012, 8). These states of mind blend the cognitive with the affective.

The field of rhetoric and composition's ambivalence toward emotion and its association with the personal is further reflected in the field's turn away from studying expressive writing in recent decades in favor of more social models of writing and rhetoric (Goldblatt 2017). However, other fields—especially clinical psychology and medicine—continue to explicitly investigate expressive writing, including its therapeutic potential to "promote insight, healing, and wellbeing" (Ruini and Mortara 2022, 23). There is considerable clinical research about expressive writing's uses to address problems including PTSD, substance use disorders, and mood disorders, as well as for palliative care and to augment medical treatment of cancer, chronic pain, HIV, COVID-19, and other physical illnesses (Gerger et al. 2021; Glass et al. 2019; Guo 2023; Reinhold, Bürkner, and Holling 2018; Ruini and Mortara 2022; Suhr, Risch, and Wilz 2017).

Discourse about journaling for mental health is ubiquitous in popular culture, and several adult students invoke the terms "therapeutic" and "cathartic" when discussing their uses of writing to "move through" difficult emotional states. When they use words like "expressing," "purging," and "clearing," they point to a drive to move the feelings outside of themselves that is consistent with societal recognition of this role for writing. For example, Tamara Vanie's characterization of journaling during a hard pregnancy is a classic use of expressive writing to write down and move through difficult feelings. She says, "My husband bought me a journal because I was just in a bad mood all the time. He was like, you need to write, you know, write down how you're feeling and how you're getting through this." The directional markers she uses, "down" and "through," appear with frequency, as does "out" in interviews with many others, thus indicating how writing facilitates both the movement of emotion and the writer's movement through emotion.

Genres researched in the scholarship of therapeutic writing range from reflective journaling to poetry and songwriting. The writing that adult students report as therapeutic includes these genres; however, they are not clinically prescribed. They are instead self-initiated—or in Tamara's case, suggested by a spouse. These writers who seek to move their powerful feelings do so through journaling, memoir, poetry, songwriting, choreography, and fiction. Several examples show additional nuance to the ways adult students exert agency through expressive writing to know their own emotions and to transform the emotional climate for themselves and others.

Writing Is a Mode of Feeling

Paula Thacker recalls developing the capacity for expressive writing independently, from a young age, in response to bullying:

> I remember, in elementary, I was going through a lot of bullying about my weight, about my hair, about my lips, just my dark skin, all kinds of things. So I used to just write, and I would just write my feelings, and write how I felt. . . . I just find that that's a way to express myself, a way to tell how I'm feeling sometimes. If you're nervous, or if you're angry, or if you're sometimes

> too excited, if the person can't get it out. But sometimes I feel like it's just a better way for me to express myself than to just say it. Because sometimes when I say it, it doesn't come out right, but when I write it, I can fully express myself, and say the things that I want.

Paula uses language that evokes outward movement, "express" and "get it out." Other phrasing, however, suggests another function of writing. Not only is it a means for moving emotion out of the body, but it also seems to be a mode of feeling in itself. When she says, "I would just write my feelings," the fusion between writing and feeling is marked by the absence of a preposition. There is no "out," "about," or "through" mediating between writing and feeling in this phase. Thacker also characterizes writing as "a way to tell how I'm feeling." While this could be interpreted as telling to others, the absence of a prepositional phrase suggests that writing is a way that the writer can tell how she's feeling.

I propose, therefore, that writing is a mode of feeling. This is analogous to Emig's theory that writing is a unique mode of learning, by which learning occurs during and through the act of writing (1977). This foundational cognitive concept of writing-to-learn provided a theoretical basis for the writing across the curriculum movement in the 1970s that continues through the cross-disciplinary uptake of reflective writing for metacognitive awareness. An emotional parallel is evident in the ways Paula Thacker and others speak about their writing. The fullness of emotion sometimes becomes specific, and knowable, through the act of writing.

This phenomenon is also evident in Lisa Fakir's experience. Lisa discusses writing during her night shifts at Duke Hospital to work through a painful period in her family life:

> I used to take . . . sheets of blank paper and staple them together because writing at that point was catharsis. It was a catharsis for me. I had a lot going on, on the inside, after my divorce from my ex-husband and I needed to just get it all out. So, literally there's a bag somewhere in my house where there's thick sheets of copy paper, stapled together from the jar (sorry Duke). But, at night because I worked third shift, I had to get it out. So, there's big letters and there's drawings and then there's scribble and then there's little tiny things. And I wrote the way I needed to write to just put something on paper so that I wouldn't misdirect my anger or frustration or depression onto my children. . . . I didn't know any other way to do it.

In the expressive discourse of "catharsis" and "get it out," and in the urgently improvised journal cobbled together from office supplies during her graveyard shift, Lisa, like Paula, chooses her own medium for moving, and moving through, troubling emotion. Her cathartic writing facilitates the emotional competence aspect of the psychological model of emotional agency in that Lisa expresses and grapples with the scope of her feelings through the act of writing. The fact that she "didn't know any other way" than writing to do this emotional work suggests the uniqueness of writing as a mode of feeling. Her case also illustrates a second dimension of writing's relationship to emotional agency. Lisa's act of redirecting emotion away from her children is a rhetorical-emotional action, an effort to influence a group's emotional environment. It is common to think of rhetorical action as directed to an audience other than the writer, but Lisa's writing achieves emotional rhetoricity without anybody else reading it when she uses writing to reroute emotional energy—the anger, frustration, and depression that she speaks of—thus influencing the emotional climate of her family. Her example of journaling shows how all parts of psychological emotional agency—the capacity to recognize, express, and influence emotion—can be enacted through writing as a mode of feeling.

Journaling is a characteristic genre for writing through emotions without worrying about an external audience, yet Gary Lassiter speaks about fiction writing as his mode for transforming emotion. He uses his stories to alter his own emotions, to gain feelings of control, and to define his sense of self. From childhood on, Gary explains, "I've never had a period where I'm not writing." In addition to writing for school and work, he has also written songs, poetry, and horror fiction. He calls horror writing a means "to escape from, but also deal" with traumatic events. He explains the genesis of this writing: "Being a product of trauma, particularly, there's certain ways you can respond to it. For me, I kinda internalized a lot of things, and for me to process everything, I turned them into stories. . . . . I would escape into books when things were happening, and that would be my world, and then, I started to want to create my own, like that wasn't good enough anymore. I want my own worlds, where I control the things because you don't have control outside of yourself." Gary characterizes reading as escape but writing as transformation. By "turning them into stories," Gary asserts agency over traumatic events and relationships. Through this same act, he also invents a self who has control over his own identity. He tells me: "A lot of my early years were defined by me playing different roles for people, but when I'm writing, I don't have to. I can just be anybody . . . I can be anybody I want."

By crafting fictionalized horror scenes, Gary expresses the harm he endures. Remarkably, even as a child, Gary also mitigates that harm by authoring a self with control over how the narrative happens and who he is in the storyline. Collins posits self-definition as an act of survival and resistance with particular importance to Black women (2000). Fiction enables Gary to adopt this strategy himself out of dire need. A written self who is "anybody I want" stands in sharp contrast to his damaging experiences of "playing different roles for [other] people." Gary thus makes visible the possibilities for writers to use self-sponsored writing to develop emotional agency, even from a very young age and especially under adverse conditions. Like Paula Thacker, who turns to journaling and writing poetry to deal with racist bullying in elementary school, Gary Lassiter also finds his own way toward the genres and writing practices that afford him a sense of self and empowerment over harmful situations that are otherwise out of his control.

Putting Emotion into Circulation

Lisa's and Gary's cases offer individualized responses to a question posed by Ahmed: "How do emotions work through texts not only to 'show' the effects of injustice, in the form of wounds and injury, but also to open up the possibility of restoration, repair, healing and recovery?" (2014, 190) Ahmed's interests in emotion and texts are, however, not so much about healing on a personal level. It is at the systemic, institutional scale where her ideas are most salient. Micciche's work on circulation identifies how emotion can move on this larger scale, positing "emotion as emerging relationally, in encounters between people, so that emotion takes form *between* bodies rather than residing *in* them" (2007, 13). Both Micciche's and Ahmed's concepts pertain to the emotional agency enacted through Adrienne Long's writings. In emails and other transactional genres, Adrienne achieves strategic circulation of emotion to catalyze action as an advocate for herself and other adult students.

I introduced Adrienne in chapter 2 as a research partner, a student organizer at NCCU, and a participant in my study of adult students' writing lives. In the situations discussed in this chapter, Adrienne uses writing as a means for expression, resistance, and advocacy, all of which are fueled by and further circulate emotion. Adrienne's rhetorical response to situations that cause harm to her and other adult students illustrates writing's value for collectively generating the emotional energy necessary to make institutional change. As I analyze the cases she offers, I make an imperfect analogy between racism and ageism in higher education because in Adrienne's actions to resist ageist practices at NCCU, she employs strategies that Black feminists and other scholars of color elucidate as modes of antiracism. For example, Adrienne treats emotion—particularly anger—as a logical response to injustice that is "loaded with information and energy" (Lorde 1984, 127). In founding a formal group for adult students, she also forges a "homeplace" within which otherwise isolated learners can tell their experiences in a "community of resistance" to ageist practices at the university (hooks 2015, 42). These two approaches for centering adult students within an institutional culture that marginalizes them are grounded in racial knowledge of how to survive and how to create change under adverse conditions, and how to leverage emotion for these purposes.

When I met her, Adrienne had recently reenrolled at NCCU after a thirty-year hiatus. She had been excited to get started. However, a campus event left Adrienne feeling "isolated" and "disappointed" before setting foot in her classes. As she began her studies, she noticed many ways that adult students like herself were marginalized in the institutional culture. These observations and emotions catalyzed her. She subsequently organized her peers and summoned support from those with more institutional power to establish the Adult Learner Student Organization (ALSO). The group gained formal status as a university-sponsored student organization just six months after Adrienne was readmitted. She achieved this while taking a full-time courseload, working two jobs, and being present for her young adult children during an academic year that was dramatically disrupted by a pandemic.

These actions were set into motion during the summer before her classes started; Adrienne attended a day-long orientation at the university that left her feeling the opposite of welcomed and oriented. She told me: "I didn't get what was promised to me. I didn't get a T-shirt, I didn't get lunch, I didn't get good advising, I didn't get a tour of the campus. I felt ill prepared walking through the door, and I felt defeated, and I felt like I didn't want to go to that school." Furthermore, Adrienne had been billed $225 for this event that met neither her expectations to become more prepared for the semester nor her desire to feel encouraged as an adult student. These feelings spotlighted the need for change. "I knew that some things needed to be addressed," she tells me, "at least from the adult learners' standpoint."

Other adult students also report intense emotions about orientations, especially when these events seem pitched only for young students. Felicia Stratton is among those who look back on orientation with feeling: "I had to lose an entire day of work to do orientation, sitting around, hanging around, having to wait for this test to happen and that test. . . . It made me angry. I was mad, I was spitting nails. I was like, 'Why am I here? This does not apply to me.' . . . If you lose one hundred bucks in a day, that's a big chunk. And to feel angry and frustrated with it, that's not helpful." Felicia moves from spitting nails to spitballing ideas for improvements. She believes NCCU could better address adult students who might be juggling parenting and jobs along with school. She wants to see what she calls "a non-seventeen-year-old orientation where we look at things like childcare, transportation, work schedules, money." Her intellectual activity of idea-generation is fueled by rather than separate from strong emotions of anger and frustration.

Actions are also motivated by emotion. Rhonda,[1] who had been an Army medic in Afghanistan, experiences such discouragement during a nursing program orientation that she takes up the matter with a department chair:

> Last semester, I was invited to an orientation for nursing and I got my packet taken out of my hand. "Give me that, you're not ready to sign up for—." I didn't have enough credits to apply for the nursing program because I still had a couple of sciences left, but it was hundreds of people that were in the auditorium, and you're going to single me out? To try to discourage me right before I'm trying to do something. I didn't need to hear that.
>
> So after she did that, I had to have a meeting with the department chair because I didn't want her to make any other veteran feel the way she made me feel. That was my whole goal. I wasn't trying to get nothing out of it. I just wanted to speak up and stand up for everybody else, and I did.

Feelings of isolation, disappointment, defeat, anger, and discouragement illuminate what matters to Adrienne, Felicia, and Rhonda about their alienating orientation experiences. All shift from personal frustration about their own treatment at these events to identifying themselves as a class of students—veterans for Rhonda, "non-seventeen-year-olds" for Felicia, and adult learners for Adrienne—groups for whom this treatment is also unacceptable. They feel, and they feel for their fellow students. It is a short step for these women to move from personal discouragement to desire for specific repairs that would improve the university for others like themselves.

Exigency Is a Feeling

There is an energetic dimension to emotional agency that is useful for thinking about emotion's role in rhetorical action. Sociologists Weenink and Spaargaren assert that "agency resides in emotions" (61) and that people are "set into motion by emotion" (2016, 62). This movement starts when emotions "light up what matters" (67), contributing to the creation of rhetorical exigency. Lorde, too, sees emotion as such a "spotlight" (1984, 124) on what matters. Adrienne's and Rhonda's rhetorical activity suggests that even emotions associated with low energy can catalyze action. Stenberg discusses a feminist process that transforms an emotion from debilitating to "the impetus for cultural critique and self-examination" (2015, 63). She argues that this act of repurposing "requires severing [emotion's] strict ties to the individual to instead approach it as a catalyst to investigate the social conditions that give rise to it" (2015, 62–63). However, Black feminist theorists help integrate individual and social concepts of emotional agency because they affirm the possibilities for personal agency while engaging with the systemic. For instance, Collins identifies "working for social change [as] an important path to personal dignity and individual freedom" (2019, 168). She anchors this in histories of Black civil society in which "fighting on behalf of freedom and social justice for the entire Black community and for a more inclusive society based on social justice was, in effect, fighting for one's own personal freedom. The two could not be easily separated"

(169). Lorde notes how emotion functions in this dialectic between the individual and the institution: "Every woman has a well-stocked arsenal of anger potentially useful against those oppressions, personal and institutional, which brought that anger into being. Focused with precision it can become a powerful source of energy serving progress and change" (1984, 127). Other scholars' concepts of emotional energy account for the spark and intensity needed to move from feeling to action in a given situation. Weenink and Spaargaren, examining the social dimensions of emotional energy, suggest it can be collectively generated in "situational solidarity" (75), an apt approach when an individual determines that their feelings are indicative of an institutional problem that affects many. This is evident in Adrienne's actions after orientation. She seeks redress for herself, and like Rhonda, she wants to influence the quality of future orientations for other adult students. On an even larger scale, she hopes to affect the campus's policies and culture toward more age-inclusivity. To do so, she sets emotion into motion through connecting with students who might share her experiences and writing to university personnel who might care to support them. Micciche refers to such desire for change as "politicized emotion, or emotion ignited and given purpose by political reality" (2005, 177). This corresponds with Ahmed's theorizing about possibilities for emotion to work through texts to open pathways for repair after injustice on institutional scales (2014). That is what Adrienne sought.

Schooling the University

During the months following her unsatisfying orientation, Adrienne opens such pathways by unleashing politicized emotion during multiple rhetorical acts that include strategic emails to university personnel. Writing with emotional agency enables her to develop a collegial relationship with a new administrator and establish a formal organization within the university to serve as a space of belonging and advocacy for adult students. This student group becomes a locus of situational solidarity that furthers Adrienne's capacities to respond strategically, with emotion, to university events and policies that have disproportionate consequences for adult learners. Adrienne's selected cases of emotional agency illuminate strategies for writing with politicized emotion. To unpack these situations requires considering the interplay between the writer, the identities she forges for herself, the texts she creates, the people she involves, and the contexts and cultures her writing draws upon and intervenes in. Circulation of emotion through written and interpersonal communication is part of the full package of rhetorical resources that Adrienne deploys to educate members of the university about how to treat adult students.

The rhetorical-emotional knowledge she enacts includes empathy for the professionals she seeks to persuade. This is characteristic of other adult students whose familiarity with workplace cultures results in their ability to imagine what it may be like to be in the shoes of university employees. For instance, during an adult student focus group, participants raise concerns about aspects of the system that are difficult for them, but they also express compassion toward the workers who try to help because of their awareness of the factors that make those jobs difficult. One notes, "Most of the people I encountered really cared and were trying their best . . . They were doing the best they could with what they had, because I know they're always cutting the Title III funds and stuff." I have written elsewhere about the historic underfunding that HBCUs face and how this disproportionate austerity affects university programs and personnel (Fulford 2019). Adult HBCU students are often aware of the economic constraints on their institution that cause system failures and thus lapses in service. Another focus group attendee observes:

> I was very proactive about it, but I had a little bit of difficulty navigating the financial aid situation . . . And I'd go down into their igloos of stacks of papers where there's one person working with looked like a thousand students worth of stuff. I'd go, "It seems like maybe some interns or someone else can help?" I would ask a really pointed question, I'd say, "It seems like you have a lot of people and everyone's working day and night, but is this enough people to deal with the situation?" . . . They were just horribly understaffed in there and when I say igloos of paper, it looked like a cartoon of a person working in an office. I was like "Don't you have a place to put this stuff? Where are the other people helping with this?" It was just this one lady.

This observer not only expresses compassion but also shows the duality of adult students' positions. They are students seeking services like any others. They are also astute, experienced members of the wider workforce who can perceive the systemic problems that interfere with university personnel being able to provide these services.

One incongruous aspect of higher education for adult learners is the generally subordinate positioning of students. This is a residue of the paternalistic philosophy of *in loco parentis* that regards young adult undergraduates as the norm and thus students in general as not yet developmentally ready to self-govern (Lake 1999; Patel 2019). This ideology competes with beliefs that most college students, being over the age of seventeen, are legally adults and are therefore agents of their own behavior and learning (Lee 2011). At NCCU, policies based on an *in loco parentis* philosophy are justified by administrators who strive to meet benchmarks for retention and completion rates under adverse conditions. The philosophy is evident in intrusive advising practices, selected curriculum inflexibilities, and other institutional norms that position the university personnel as more knowledgeable than students about what is in students' best interests. This administrative stance can rankle seasoned adults who are accustomed to exercising agency in their own interests. When the role of undergraduate is overly associated with youth, adult students may struggle to assert more agentive identities in their interactions with personnel.

Adrienne holds these dual undergraduate and professional subjectivities as she advocates for adult students, and she is sensitive to the interpersonal complexities this may cause in a hierarchical institution predominantly shaped for less experienced learners. In this context, Adrienne creates a unique role for herself that tacitly rejects subordination by grafting her authoritative adult identity onto the subject position of student. This move echoes Gary Lassiter's authoring of an agentive self in the face of roles others harmfully subject him to, and it offers a vivid example of Black feminist self-definition tailored for a higher education context (Collins 2000). Adrienne's strength-based remaking of a hybrid student/adult identity is evident in her emails to staff, faculty, and the chancellor, as is the complexity of crafting this identity in ways that are emotionally strategic, assertive yet nonthreatening. When writing to university personnel, Adrienne demonstrates respect for the organization's structures and individuals' areas of responsibility, acknowledging her role as student. Yet she eschews a diffident stance in her communications with all these readers. Instead, her writing projects confidence that she is coming from a particular standpoint that affords a valuable perspective, one that the reader should find informative toward meeting their own objectives.

Adrienne treats the university something like a workplace; she invents a distinctive institutional role for herself as a member who is both a student and a free agent professional who sets her own agenda for improving the university. This approach enables her to supplant or at least overlay the institutionally subordinate identity of student with a more empowered adult identity. In some instances, Adrienne offers peer-like collaborative assistance to campus personnel in solving the problems she highlights, thus bringing her adult capabilities to the forefront of communications. In these ways, Adrienne positions herself as a quasi-colleague who is poised to work with her correspondents as an active agent for changes that will be beneficial for her, other adult students, and her readers in meeting their responsibilities within the institution. This is an agentive approach by which Adrienne resists subordination to other campus adults (staff, faculty, and senior administrators). While identifying the need for personnel to function with a more inclusive operational definition of "student," she simultaneously resists assimilation into a generic student body by arguing for (and modeling) the distinctiveness of the adult student population. This is another form of self-definition, but on a collective scale. She accomplishes this through exercising emotional agency in her campus communications, both written and interpersonal. In these exchanges, she acknowledges that adult students need resources, guidance, and sound policy from the university, but she points out how these may be different from those that are applicable to younger students. Her emotionally informed discourse calls for university personnel to resee the undergraduate population more inclusively and therefore to rethink their responsibilities to the full student body. Adrienne leverages decades of communicative experiences to accomplish this complex messaging.

Chief among Adrienne's written interventions is email. Professionals in chapter 4 show that this mundane genre can be used as a tool for effecting equity in workplaces. Although school is not her workplace, Adrienne's advocacy emails at the university repurpose her considerable professional writing experience. She uses email to circulate emotional energy when the institution's actions have adverse effects on her and other adult students. Two emails written seven months apart, the first to a program director, the second to the chancellor, reveal Adrienne's approaches for diplomatically schooling the university about this population. She initiates the first in the fall while the adult student organization that she eventually establishes is little more than a promising idea. It is a formally recognized campus entity by the time she writes to the chancellor the following summer.

In early November, three months after she begins classes, Adrienne crafts an email to a recently hired program administrator whose responsibilities include orientation. This email is one of many "sow the seed" actions that Adrienne takes that fall to try to build a network of staff and faculty who might become advocates for adult students. The email to Dr. O[2] intervenes in a delicate rhetorical situation in that Adrienne wants the message to serve multiple purposes: "It was an introduction of who I am and really what I wanted to talk to her about, my personal experience, and then I also wanted to share with her some of the work that I was starting to do with adult learning and get her by it. So whether she wanted to hear what I had to say or not, at least she knew that something was on the rise." Because the email also seeks a remedy for orientation's failures, Adrienne has to walk a fine line between critic and potential collaborator. Adrienne hopes this email will secure a meeting with Dr. O at which she can more thoroughly do what she calls "a sales pitch" about supporting and collaborating with adult learners.

Email is a ubiquitous transactional genre. Unlike horror fiction, journals, and poetry, email does not seem like the kind of writing that evokes emotion. However, Adrienne's approach to this workaday genre affirms that it can be a vehicle for circulating emotion that draws upon many traditions. Adrienne invokes both family and workplace cultures when she explains how she crafts correspondence. She regards important emails as letters, and she repurposes her family's practices of letter writing and storytelling to fully develop them. Adrienne also has copious professional experience with email due to past employment at large corporations. She estimates that she has responded to hundreds of messages per day at several jobs. She refers to her past job training about corporate communication. From her workplaces, she knows that—for better or for worse—email can circulate beyond the intended recipient, and it is discoverable in legal disputes. She has been directed to use email as a "CYA" (Cover Your Ass) method, and to combine it with face-to-face and phone interactions for maximum effect. She has long familiarity with the rhetorical flexibility required of the genre: "I particularly pride myself on email writing. . . . If I really take my time with it . . . I can be very diplomatic and nice-nasty . . . at one time. I pride myself on being able to keep the peace and get my message across and doing either softly or firmly." Although she still feels strongly about the failures of orientation, she approaches her correspondence about the problems strategically, taking extra care with the substance and tone of her email because she is not just seeking correctives for her own experience at orientation. She is seeking to establish relationships across campus with people who have power to alter how the institution regards adult students. With the stakes that high, Adrienne carefully weighs how to craft her first email to Dr. O: "Sometimes emails take me a day or so. I'll write the whole email and leave it in draft and then come back, because this email in particular . . . there was some level of passion. Gritty passion is still there. It hadn't been refined at that point. It was a lot of thinking, a lot of empathy, a lot of information, a lot of clouds because I didn't know who all the players were, just a lot of figuring out, really, should I send this? What should my tone be? I want it to be respectful."

How (Not) to Orient Adult Students. The exigence for Adrienne's email is spotlit by her initial emotional response to orientation. However, months after the precipitating event, she diffracts her discouragement into a series of emotion-informed rhetorical moves that simultaneously call out the university and offer expert insider assistance in designing future events.

> SOARS ORIENTATION
> Wed, Nov 6, 2019, 9:52 P.M.
>
> Hello Dr._____,
>
> My name is Adrienne Long and I'm a sophomore re-admit student here at NCCU. I got your name from Mr.______, who is in charge of the Transfer Student Association. After expressing my concern with the SOAR program I attended this past summer, he suggested that I reach out to you. He explained that you've recently taken charge of this department and that your office is working to understand ways to improve or revamp your program. I asked him if you had a Student Advisory board that would be working to assist you as you move forward over the next year. I'm currently working with the staff of the Transfer Office to start a club for our Non-Traditional students. So far, we are in the beginning phase of organizing a club that will address the needs of adult

learners (24+ aged). Additionally, having an opportunity during SOARS to network with other 24+ adults, learn what's expected as a student, new technology (apps/Banner/Blackboard), understanding the services we pay for (i.e., campus shuttle, etc..) would be a HUGE benefit. Continuing the support beyond orientation is the goal of the Adult Learner club which would be to provide peer-to-peer mentoring, help with assimilation, provide adult on/off-campus activities (student and family friendly) networking, advocacy and community service efforts. We too are students and want to be included and feel a part of the campus, whether studying on-line or commuting. I want to ensure that future students succeed by minimizing the stress of worrying about fitting in or understanding how to navigate the campus and technological services. The concerns I've received so far from my peers could directly impact the improvement of the SOARS program and help create a supportive environment for adult students ensuring a good start and successful completion. I'm returning back to school after being out for over 30 years and not knowing what I should know has prevented me from participating in activities of interest or at times left me feeling very alone in this journey.

Not to mention, I contacted the school over the summer and was promised that ALL of my questions and concerns would be addressed during SOARS. Sadly that didn't happen, nor the promise of a tee-shirt or lunch fulfilled. Some feedback from the two day interest reception we hosted provided direct feedback regarding the SOARS orientation, which indicated that I wasn't alone in my experience or disappointment. I'd personally like to be refunded as I don't believe that the cost of attending provided any benefit whatsoever. Additionally, when I inquired about what the cost covered, I couldn't get a direct answer only that cost couldn't be refunded. I was offered a "hardship" which meant billing my account instead of paying out of pocket up front. I have student loans so it concerns me that I am possibly financing my "hardship".

I'd love the opportunity to speak with you directly to understand the mission/goals of your office as well as offer ANY assistance as a student with addressing the needs of our adult students.

Kind regards,
Adrienne Long

The moves Adrienne makes include crafting a fluid position for herself and projecting a collegial one upon her reader. She navigates their respective areas of authority and signals the reader's responsibility without directly casting blame. By stating that she has heard that Dr. O has only "recently taken charge of this department," and is "working to understand ways to improve," Adrienne offers a little grace, implying that the orientation problems may have been inherited and unintended, but they now need tending; she crafts a reader who is already moving in that direction. She also judiciously distributes emotive vocabulary into the email only after starting from a neutral and informative stance. The subject line "SOARS Orientation" gives nothing away about the feelings that prompted the email. The only indication in the first 200 words that this might be a complaint letter is the phrase "expressing my concern," in the third sentence, but this is stated in a relatively neutral tone surrounded by informative prose about a nascent club for adult learners and related seed-planting of the idea for a student advisory board. Adrienne aligns herself with the transfer office, using the plural "we" to indicate that her efforts are university-sponsored already at this "beginning phase of organizing." Gradual inclusion of more marked language signifies an emotion-informed analysis of the past to highlight what needs to change about orientation and the university's other interactions with adult students. "We too are students and want to be included," documents a collective longing for belonging that is as yet unmet; the phrase is a precursor to what will eventually become the student organization's assertive, self-defining motto: "We are ALSO students." But that group is not yet formed, so Adrienne can speculate but not yet write with the full authority of the collective. In the final sentence of the first long paragraph, she shows herself to be one student "feeling very alone in this journey" before the next paragraph points out how orientation specifically failed her.

The warm one-sentence closing paragraph positions the reader and the writer in future alliance, with Adrienne no longer the lone complainant but instead an adult poised to understand and assist, albeit humbly "as a student," yet with the two engaged in "addressing the needs of our adult students." The "our" here could be Adrienne and Dr. O or it could refer to NCCU's overall culture, including them both. Regardless, to address the needs that Adrienne delineates is a shared responsibility. Adrienne's email conveys that adult students are poised to do it for themselves, they just need a bit more cooperation from university personnel like Dr. O.

This email achieves an almost immediate response, with an invitation sent the next morning to talk. When they meet, Adrienne learns that Dr. O had been an adult learner, too, as a doctoral student. Even so, "I just don't think she was aware of the possible experience at the undergraduate level. . . . She wasn't really thinking about it in terms of the challenges that we face day to day. . . . I went through the [orientation] experience with her and highlighted some ways that we could really try to help a student like myself who felt misguided and really treated badly during that time." Adrienne uses her own emotion-saturated situation as a case indicative of a larger pattern, something that she and Dr. O can analyze together as problem-solvers. This quasi-colleague stance persists when she talks about the aims for a successful orientation, inclusive of adult learners: "Let's get them pumped and amplified about the opportunity and make them feel wanted." The "us" is Adrienne and Dr. O; the "them" is the next group of adult learners to experience orientation. Emotion stays present during this alliance-building meeting, Adrienne reports: "It was such a strong connection. It was a really good meeting. We hugged each other. There was a few tears." The emotional agency Adrienne enacts through both written and in-person communication with this administrator enables her to point the way to orientations pitched for all NCCU's undergraduates.

How (Not) to Communicate Policy Changes. The second situation I examine begins June 2021 with the university administration's decision to return to in-person instruction for the fall after going fully remote during the first year of the pandemic. This was not a local decision alone; it was a response to system-wide policy. However, the communication choices by the university administration left many students unaware and unprepared for the dramatic changes in the fall. Scrambling to meet the system's mandate, the university abruptly changed students' fall schedules with neither advance communication nor new advising sessions. Adrienne notes that there was only one announcement about the changes. It was buried in students' summer emails with a throwaway subject line. She almost missed it. When she finally opened it and saw her revised schedule, she was devastated. None of the other students in ALSO noticed it until she forwarded it to them.

Adrienne's vocabulary about her feelings at this moment indicates the intensity and breadth of her emotional response; she called the decision "devastating," "catastrophic," and "urgent." She felt "appalled," "shocked," "desperate," "defensive," and "upset." Mainly, she was angry, and not just for herself: "I was angry for all of us. This can't be. I was in disbelief, truthfully." There was no way Adrienne could continue her studies with the unilaterally revised schedule. It conflicted too profoundly with all her other adult responsibilities. The graduation she had sacrificed so much for would be set back indefinitely. Adrienne's initial communications with the offices of advising and online instruction did not remedy the situation.

Other members of ALSO were similarly affected. Adrienne broadcast information to this group by all means she could think of, including forwarding the university's email, posting alerts on their social media groups and group chat, and calling an online meeting of the organization to discuss the ramifications for members. "This really broke my heart," she said, voicing perspectives she heard from working parents in particular, who found their newly imposed class schedules impossible: "Okay, so now that I have to go back in person, I have kids that are home taking remote school. How am I going to work that out? My job is allowing me to be at home. The kids in school have to be home. I was taking school at home, and now you're asking me to be at school all day two days a week or three days. How's that work?" Her contact with these peers amplified and focused the emotional energy regarding the university's policy. Fueled by her anger and the group's shared frustrations, Adrienne drafted a nearly 1,300-word email to the university's chancellor, plus attachments with further documentation, in which she conveyed the urgency of the problem. She explains the connections between thinking and feeling as she wrote this high-stakes correspondence: "I just turned anger fuel into something productive. And that's why I handled it all with care because I could have come off as just angry, which I was. That's all I really felt was just really defensive and just really upset. But then to bring it all back, it was like, 'You're dealing with adults, get them to think. Get them to put themselves in your shoes, get them to take some responsibility.'" The email she writes is a strategic work of emotional rhetorical power designed to swiftly move the chancellor from one position to another. Adrienne knew she needed to "evoke some emotion" so that the chancellor would feel accountable. She explains her opening strategy for conveying urgency: "I was desperate. It was very strategic in my head like, 'I have to capture his attention. This is more than just an email from anybody, this is important. You need to stop, drop and roll. Read this, even if it's spam. You see the word IMPORTANT in that subject? You need to know this is coming from somebody important, and this is important.' That was my immediate feeling. And that's why I did that." Adrienne's strikingly informative subject line, "IMPORTANT: the catastrophic effect on adult learners with the recent class schedule changes," stands in sharp contrast to the overlook-able summer email from the university about these changes. That was intentional: "I wanted my email to look different than their email looked because that's what their email should have said. 'Important.' And it didn't." Adrienne models the art of the subject line, schooling the university on how to communicate time-sensitive information that has critical ramifications for its readers.

The substance of the email further informs the chancellor of the consequences for adult students of their hastily implemented policy. She layers emotional elements with logical evidence. Adrienne makes a direct appeal to the chancellor, requesting "compassion and understanding" for adult students. She explains who she is as an active, high-achieving student and founder of the Adult Learner Student Organization. She describes her anticipation about making her family proud at the December graduation, a goal that was in sight before the university's abrupt policy change. She describes the significant economic and emotional hardship that will result from delayed graduation because the schedule she has been assigned is utterly misaligned with the jobs she now holds during the second grueling year of the pandemic. She documents her unsuccessful attempts to resolve the problem lower down the chain of command. "Without on-line class instruction and the Distance Learning program off the table, how am I supposed to get a return on my investment? I'm in my last semester and will not be able to transfer to another institution . . . I'm fast approaching 50 and already feel edged out of the job market with younger, brighter students competing to go into the corporate arena. I'm completely devastated that I have nowhere to turn to with this issue. How am I supposed to compete without a degree? How am I going to pay back the student loans I've obtained?" Each question she asks is designed to put the chancellor in her shoes. Her anguish is palpable in her closing, where she poses her fourth question: "This feels nothing like an American dream but a nightmare. I've spent money, worked extremely hard at school while working two jobs and will net nothing. How do I explain this to my children?" Adrienne appends this plea with her transcript and class schedule, the university's original summer email, her prior correspondence seeking help, and testimony from six other adult students who affirm the hardships imposed upon them by the university's sudden and poorly communicated change.

This time, Adrienne's email yields a cooperative response from the chancellor's delegate within twenty-four hours. Although their subsequent negotiations do not yield the systemic change she seeks of online instruction being made available for all, Adrienne does secure a pathway for herself to graduate on time and the promise from this helpful administrator to try to accommodate any other adult students she refers to them. It also seems that her firm message alerts the university to its communication failures. Months later, she tells me: "I've been getting emails about registering for classes in 2022. And the subject line and the way they're being sent out is completely different. So I bet I'm not the only one that said something."

Writing with feeling has many potential dimensions that are made evident when adult students speak about their writing lives. Paula Thacker's and Lisa Fakir's cases suggests writing is a unique mode of feeling akin to the concept of writing as a mode of thinking and learning. They and Gary Lassiter use writing as a means for repair on a personal level, with Gary's case also indicating writing's utility as a practice of self-definition. But writing with emotion also has broader social purposes, as Adrienne's cases show. Her efforts to craft an agentive student/adult identity put emotion into strategic circulation toward the transformative social change she seeks for those who share that identity.

Adrienne's activities to establish a student organization, to develop a supportive network of adult learners and university personnel, and to push back against policies and practices that do harm to adult students all demonstrate that writing is a mode for channeling emotional energy into emotional agency. Through the workaday genres of texts, group chats, social media, and email, Adrienne expresses emotion to her peers. She thus amplifies emotional energy—what she calls "anger fuel"—through situational solidarity with other students like her. She channels that collective energy into her institutional correspondence to try to move administrators to action. Feminist communication scholars offer us further conceptual framing that pertains to this dynamic interaction between a feeling individual and the system she seeks to change. Krone and Dougherty define the term "critical emotional agency" as "a morally and politically attentive set of practices that involve acknowledging, processing and acting on emotion in support of transformative social change. These include making sense of emotional experiences in ways that empower resistance, cultivate the capacity for self-determination, and strengthen the ability to act 'otherwise' within and beyond the margins of formal organizations" (2015, n.p.). Adrienne's advocacy work demonstrates that writing is among these attentive practices of critical emotional agency. She uses it to translate emotional experiences into power to resist. The circulation of emotional energy that writing facilitates amplifies her ability to act, and it ignites others to also be moved to act, creating emotion-fueled possibilities for institutional change. Emotion and reason are furthermore entwined in Adrienne's actions, neither subordinated to the other, just as her dual identities of adult and undergraduate coexist to inform her rhetorical stances.

Even when bracketing out coursework and professional writing experiences where emotion also does critical work, the cases in this chapter suggest the power of writing with emotion for personal and social change. The many emotion-informed writing practices illustrated here could become part of integrative rhetorical education that repairs the artificial schism between intellect and emotion that persists in academia. Bringing these into closer relationship within higher education is one way to respect and learn from the experiential knowledge of adult learners.

Conclusion

Learning from Adult Learners

The summer before she graduated, Adrienne Long worked on an adult student research team whose investigations included searching for representations of adult learners and HBCU students in popular culture. Ever since that project, Adrienne has been in the habit of sending me news about adult students. This isn't often; it can be two to eight months between her messages because, as her research team discovered, representations of students like themselves are negligible in popular media. The headlines for the stories Adrienne finds have a dramatic angle to them: "68-Year-Old [white] Woman Graduates, Named Valedictorian at Kentucky's HBCU After Growing Up in Segregation."[1] "101-Year-Old Woman Returned to School and Will Graduate College With Her Granddaughter This Year."[2] "Mother Gets Pregnant at 13; Her Son Dropped Out of High School at 16; Both Get PhDs at the Same Time."[3] Catchy graduation stories like these, about outliers overcoming long odds, are among the phenomena that Adrienne's team uncovered when scouring popular media for any representations of adult students. The other major phenomenon they discovered is recruitment ads. These are primarily for online institutions, an indicator of the enrollment stratification I document in chapter 1. Albeit limited, these kinds of media do provide images of diverse adults achieving their educational goals. However, they represent these students only at the bookends of the academic experience. Over the long studious period between recruitment and graduation, news and entertainment media, and even university communications offices, overwhelmingly represent college life as the domain of the young.

The work of this book therefore begins simply by centering adult students. My initial goal with this approach was to understand more about this population and their writing. Yet perhaps the more consequential findings come from investigating aspects of higher education from adult students' standpoints. The forthrightness of students made this expansion of research outcomes possible. Adult-centered co-inquiry yields three interrelated sets of lessons from adult learners that are interspersed through the chapters. The first set of lessons is about higher education. The lessons call into question common educational ideologies and the practices based upon them. They also offer adult-inclusive alternatives to these marginalizing beliefs. The second set of lessons is for researchers interested in studying adult students. These lessons suggest heterogeneous, flexible research approaches in keeping with the nature of this population. From design through dissemination, researching about and with adult students can take distinctive forms. Thirdly and finally, my aim of understanding adult students' writing lives simultaneously yields field-expanding theoretical understandings about the nature of writing due to the breadth of these students' experiential knowledge.

Lessons about Higher Education

Placing adults at the center of educational inquiry shines a spotlight on what's missing from the prevailing idea of the college student in American culture. Other common educational concepts do not hold up well under this reframing, either. Persistence and retention discourse and college-to-career rhetoric are both shown to be conceptually incomplete when juxtaposed with the lives of the adult students profiled in this book. Out of critical analysis come lessons for change.

Expanding the Idea of the Student

Dominant ideologies about college students as unencumbered post–high schoolers contribute to the tendencies of faculty, staff, and administrators to overlook adult students as integral members of a student body whose experiences, needs, array of responsibilities, and capacities to contribute differ from their younger classmates. Even former adult students such as myself and Dr. O have difficulty shifting our tacit conception of "students" to an age-inclusive definition because of the normative ideologies that permeate our professional lives. As Adrienne Long and others teach us, our institutions often do not seem well-informed about adult learners even when this group comprises a significant proportion of a school's students. As with racism, classism, and other oppressive forces, confronting ageism in higher education requires deliberate self-education and resistant action against everyday practices that reproduce inequity.

Many who are profiled in this book resist ageist norms in higher education. They advocate for themselves and other adult students. Their personal experiences show them that they are members of an overlooked group; they want university personnel to recognize that adult students are an important part of the whole student population. An aspiring nursing student alerted a program chair that her staff were not yet adequately informed about pathways for veterans. At a national conference, Stuart Parrish suggested to diversity, equity, and inclusion staff that age diversity belongs in the matrix of student identities that they serve. Adrienne Long created anti-ageist messaging through her Adult Learner Student Organization by repeatedly insisting that adult learners are *also* students.

We cannot leave this reeducation responsibility just on the shoulders of students. Creating age-diverse institutional cultures requires solidarity across students and personnel. We are jointly responsible for changing the beliefs and practices that exclude adults from full participation in academic life. However, students can take the lead on identifying priorities because they have firsthand emotional knowledge of exclusionary practices. We must learn from them.

A Holistic Model of Persisting

One of the ageist practices tethered to normative ideas about students is comparative measurement of student persistence, retention, and graduation rates, a practice that pits institutions against each other in the competition for rankings and funding. As chapter 3 discusses, the definition of persistence in accountability metrics privileges continuous college enrollment for three semesters, which is not always a realistic goal for students like Stuart Parrish and Tamara Vanie, who nevertheless do persist on their own terms and time frames across many aspects of their lives, including degree attainment. Yet their persistence does not count on any institutional benchmarking.

Normative accountability measures are a problem for institutions that serve students of any age who must juggle multiple responsibilities outside of academics. The benchmarks that these schools are held to curtail development of more flexible models of degree progression. They discourage institutions from enrolling students whose profiles make them appear to be risky prospects, who might degrade a school's rates of retention and graduation. Fixed term rhetorics of expedience, like "finish in four," "graduate on time," and "two-year program," perpetuate higher education ideologies that elide the many people whose lives preclude the efficiency privileged by neoliberalism. By standard measures, completing college over seven, ten, or forty years—or not at all—are all currently marked as failures to persist on time.

The cases in this book point to the value of developing a qualitative concept of persisting that makes space for dipping in and out of education in response to the life breadth of adults' responsibilities. For those students, like Tamara, who "continue trying over time," education is but one meaningful activity among many, which makes it difficult to quantitatively measure adult students' actual acts of persisting. However, reseeing students as persisting holistically could affect a wide spectrum of higher education practices including recruitment, advising, reenrollment policies, strategic planning, and arguments for funding, thus creating more equitable opportunities for adult students.

Multidirectional, Multidimensional Learning

The cases in the prior chapters demonstrate—as other scholars of adult learning know so well—that advanced learning is hardly the exclusive domain of colleges and universities. Adults develop knowledge from many different contexts. This is cultural knowledge. It is technical and practical know-how. It is interpersonal and self-awareness. It is rhetorical savvy. It is knowledge of craft and process. Through experience, many have developed mature ethical and emotional capacities that inform the actions they take in their homes, communities, and workplaces. This knowledge is nonstandard and not standardizable.

However, one ramification of age stereotypes about students is a common assumption that the direction of learning flows one way, up a vertical curriculum and outward from school to the workforce. This belief is evident in the prevalence of college-to-career rhetoric with which many curricular and teaching practices align. Adult students throw this model into question because they have prior and concurrent experiential knowledge that can inform their studies. Learning is not unidirectional. Skill and knowledge from academics can certainly pertain to adults' lives, and it can be usefully future oriented. Yet adults can also use their life experiences to critically evaluate the concepts they learn in academia, as Sandra did in my technical writing class. Christopher Genwright's actions in his public administration classes show that adults can bring additional professional knowledge to bear on discussions, adding dimensional nuance to principles forwarded in coursework. Adult students thus offer an alternative multidirectional, multidimensional lifespan model of learning across time and mutually informing sites of practice that is inclusive of higher education but does not place it as the starting point.

Lessons about Educational Research

Adult undergraduates' relative absence from research-oriented universities due to institutional age biases means that those scholars with the most time for research may not perceive the heterogeneous adult student population as a critical group to study. They are thus underresearched. However, this current paucity of representation affords abundant opportunities for new scholarship that could move in multiple directions because there is so much to be learned from this population. The main lesson, then, is to research adult students. There is need. Connections between ethical agency and research are apparent because addressing the gaps in representation of adult students contributes to educational equity.

Research in Relation

To invoke the theme of emotion raised by adult student writers, my experience of researching about and with this population has been joyful, energizing, moving, and unsettling—among many other feelings—and I cannot imagine doing it except in relation to members of the group that it is about. With research partnerships, the experience becomes a shared emotion-informed intellectual activity, a scholarly process that puts faculty and students into community with each other under the umbrella identity of adult learners working on behalf of other adult learners. Some of the emotional complexity of the experience comes from grappling with our differences. For example, I have to confront repeatedly the whiteness that is an impediment to doing racially just research and my feelings of inadequacy while trying anyway. Having insider coresearchers with faceted cultural knowledge helps me trust the integrity of the team so I can "stop apologizing and do the work," as Teresa Redd counseled me early in my efforts. Relational work can include interviewing approaches such as co-interpretation to honor the intersubjectivity of interlocutor and participant, as well as the use of teams comprised of insiders of varied identities and experiences who contribute a matrix of standpoints at critical stages of the work.

Rhizomatic Methodologies

The adult student population's radical heterogeneity makes standardization of research approaches challenging and sometimes beside the point. It remains important to design with a predictive mindset, to develop meaningful research questions and rational methods to seek answers. However, it is equally important to improvise approaches in response to emerging situations. Application of rhizomatic theory to adult learner research promotes this requisite methodological flexibility. This allows for multidirectional development of a project, complementary uses of traditional and less traditional analytical methods, and learning from outliers as much as from patterns. From recruitment and data collection through analysis and dissemination, qualitative researchers focusing on adult students need to be prepared to veer from a plan in order to follow where students lead.

Methodological heterogeneity is not random or chaotic, however. The choice to change direction derives from attending closely to participants and collaborators, discerning alongside them when an approach may not be fruitful and the situation calls for something different.

Lessons about Writing

I have elected to bring attention to some of the vast and varied writing that lies outside the periphery of academics rather than on what adult students produce for their coursework. My reasoning for this is twofold. First, those of us who teach adult students already have access to their academic writing, but we are generally not privy to the writing they do outside of our disciplinary contexts. Second, this is where adult students place most emphasis during their interviews about their writing lives. Although they discuss academics, they talk more about their self-directed and professional writing. This makes sense quantitatively, especially for those who have been out of college for more years than they have been in it. Their occasions for consequential rhetorical practice largely have been personal, family, community, and professional situations. There is more research to be done that examines the interplay between academic writing and these other contexts, yet there are abundant lessons we can learn about these writers, their writing, and writing more broadly by dwelling outside coursework.

Rewriting Theory

These students cast light on aspects of writing that may be less evident in assignment-based investigations of student writers. For instance, Tamara Vanie's broad uses of writing include "developing the self" while resisting racism and sexism as these affect her, her family, and her community. We see in her examples the seeds for the conceptual work that follows in subsequent chapters, about relationships between emotion and writing and how writing can be a form of ethical agency. The working adults profiled in this book demonstrate that writing on the job can be a deeply principled activity in which entanglements between personal ethics and institutional practices require savvy negotiation. Through examination of emotion-suffused situations in other writers' personal and academic lives, writing is furthermore revealed to be a mode of feeling and a means for enacting critical emotional agency, a concept that repairs the traditional separation between emotion and intellect.

Teaching Implications

The diversity of rhetorical experience that adult students draw upon has potential to transform learning environments if it is brought into conversation with academic content. I have discussed my own struggles to make space for the unscripted knowledge that adults bring to bear on the subjects I teach. Sometimes I am humbled by pushback when I present an idea that does not align with an adult student's lived experience, as when Sandra questioned my advice about instructional writing. However, that kind of corrective is as important as the elaborations on course concepts that professionals like Christopher

Genwright can offer. The point is that there is an abundance of lived knowledge about writing in the room when adult students are part of age-integrated classes. That knowledge can either be sidelined or foregrounded. The latter offers a great deal more to our academic communities.

It is necessary to confront ageism in higher education first by recognizing the cultural formations that contribute to the marginalization of adult students. Those structural elements include the radical stratification of adult students away from elite education and toward high-cost low-value options that market to them heavily but fail to provide equal opportunity education. Enrollment inequities measured by age furthermore disproportionately affect nonwhite students and poor and working-class students, resulting in compounding marginalization effects even while these students shore up enrollments at tuition-dependent institutions.

However, the cases in this book demonstrate that adult students are valuable members of our postsecondary institutions whose contributions to educational and societal equity can be amplified when we provide space for them to do so. This space can take many forms. Adults' experiential authority positions them well to serve as informal learning leaders in mixed-age classrooms where their life-tested knowledge of rhetoric, writing practices, culture, and subject areas enriches the theories and practices that we teach. Furthermore, these same experiential resources enable adult students to serve as insider partners on research that is about them, their communities, and the institutional cultures that affect them.

The egalitarian practice of co-inquiry that enriches research is an equally valuable approach for teaching and educational activism. Encouragement from responsive faculty, staff, and administrators goes a long way for the many individuals in this population. In turn, adult students have capacities to intervene where higher education's entrenched structures lag the realities of those it aims to serve. Sometimes, therefore, students are the ones to take the lead on institutional change, as chapter 5 demonstrates. We can regard adult students as resources to learn from and "get beside," as Adrienne says, as we create more equitable adult-inclusive institutional cultures.

Appendix

Demographics of Adult Student Writers across Academic Disciplines (*n*=30)

	Social sciences	Applied professions	Arts and humanities	Sciences	TOTAL
Women	6	12	1	1	20
Men	2	6	1	1	10
Black/Af Am	5	13	2	1	21
White	3	3		1	7
Asian American		1			1
Mixed race		1			1
Age 25–29	2	2	1		5
Age 30–39	3	4		2	9
Age 40–49	2	8	1		11
Age 50–59	1	4			5
Undergraduate Age 25+	7	5	2	1	15
Graduate & professional Age 30+	1	13		1	15
Total	8	18	2	2	30

Participants were asked to self-describe their gender, race/ethnicity, age, and field of study.

Acknowledgments

I am indebted to all the adult students who are represented in this book as participants and as co-researchers. They have my utmost appreciation for trusting me to do something meaningful with the stories from their lives. Many who are not directly cited have nevertheless moved me to new understandings, as have the members of NCCU's Adult Learner Student Organization who welcomed me to their meetings to discuss the research in progress. I am also thankful to students in my classes at NCCU who fired up my thinking and dialed open my heart. They showed me how valuable mixed-age classrooms are for everyone's learning, including mine. Students who took Theories of Writing or my interdisciplinary research seminar in fall 2020 kept me engaged with this research during an exceptionally strenuous semester.

Steff Frigo is a keen advocate for adult learners and my frequent coinvestigator and coauthor. Her friendship and enthusiasm for this work sustain me. The book cites several of the student researchers who have collaborated with us. The comprehensive team includes Jamal Whitted, Brandon Cutler, and Judy Spruiell, who assisted us during our study of returning adult students. Thomas Kelly and Yaseen Abdul-Malik helped me launch the writing lives study. Stuart Parrish served on both projects. Steff and I co-mentored the cross-institutional team of Charity Philips, Tessa Delgo, Catherine Winfree, and Adrienne Long during Duke's Story+ Summer Institute. This group pointed me to hotspots that I might have missed without their acuity. Steff, Adrienne, Thomas, Stuart, and Yaseen have coauthored with me on adjacent projects while I have been working on this book. Our ongoing collaboration means so much to me.

This work was supported with funding from North Carolina Central University's Office of Academic Affairs. Duke University provided funding and research time through the Humanities Unbounded Visiting Faculty Fellows, the Story+ Institute, and the Faculty Write Program. The Franklin Humanities Institute hosted my year in residence. Kemi Elufiede's invitation to the Carnegie Writers Conference helped me work out my ideas about emotion. At the Dartmouth Summer Seminar for Composition Research, I began grappling with the limitations of coding and rehearsing my arguments in defense of the outliers. I am grateful also to the Writing through the Lifespan Collaboration, especially to Talinn Phillips, Ryan Dippre, and Charles Bazerman, for fostering a community for writing researchers doing longitudinal and latitudinal studies.

Many colleagues at NCCU, Duke, and the University at Buffalo have provided just the right thing at just the right time. These include, from NCCU: Danielle Colbert-Lewis, Karen Grimwood, Frank Leggett, Kimberly Phifer-McGhee, Robert Wortham, Johnnie Sutherland, Sandra Howard, Ilean Sutton, Charmaine McKissick-Melton, Matt Cook, Brett Chambers, Tia Marie Doxey, Jeanette Barker, and Carole Montgomery. Kathryn Wymer's work with students as partners in institutional change has been particularly inspiring. At Duke, I benefited from the support of Ranjana Khanna, Gennifer Weisenfeld, Edward Balleisen, Liz Milewicz, Haley Walton, Laura Eastwood, Pamela Montgomery, and Jehanne Gheith. Sylvia Miller's publication advice and Amanda Starling Gould's inclusion of NCCU's adult student researchers at the Story+ Institute were especially powerful. The Department of English at University at Buffalo afforded me funding, research time, and most crucially, colleagues who stepped in to support the Academic and Professional Writing Program when I was in peak writing mode. Bill Solomon advocated for my research leave; Jason Maxwell, Douglas Basford, Nicholas Hoffman, and Jay Barber all helped me put a wall around my writing time by taking on extra responsibilities. Adam Drury, Emily Cooney, Andrew Burgess, Wendy Belz, Shalee Hill, and Karen Korczynski also made sure the house didn't burn down and I had what I needed. Patricia Matthew, David Alff, and Miriam Taggert gave astute feedback that helped me refine the book proposal. Paul Feigenbaum commented generously on chapter 5. Elizabeth Mazzolini, Walt Hakala, Stacy Hubbard, Carrie Bramen, and Kristin Moore encouraged me. Rachel Ablow kept me focused and on pace. Beyond the department, Melinda Whitford offered expert advice about educational data that made it possible for me to write chapter 1.

My undergraduate and graduate experiences inflect this book. While I was an adult undergraduate at Keene State College, I benefited from the age-inclusivity that I advocate. There, Judith Perry provided expert advising. Nona Fienberg integrated adult and traditional students in collaborative projects. Margaret Walsh invited me to think like a sociologist. Kirsti Sandy encouraged my first forays into rhetorical research about economic marginality. Sarah Spykman was my wry partner in deviance as the only other English major in our age bracket. It has been a minute since graduate school, yet I still carry research lessons from advisors Patt Dodds, Donna LeCourt, and Anne Herrington at University of Massachusetts, Amherst. I aspire to Anne's methodological integrity whenever I'm wrangling an ethical conundrum.

Christine Tulley's workshop on managing complex workflows and Laura Portwood-Stacer's on book proposals and editing were all perfectly pitched at key phases of this work. Monique Dufour and Jennifer Ahern-Dodson ran writing workshops that helped me find meaning and creativity in my scholarship. Nan Mullenneaux, Sandra Tarabochia, and Adam Rosenblatt inspired me with their repertoires of creative inquiry methods. Exchanging research drawings and poems with Adam gave me courage to trust this process.

Multiple writing groups sustained this project. At the early stages, I benefited from the encouragement of Andrés Fabián Henao-Castro, who lovingly organized our feedback group at the Franklin Humanities Institute. During the pandemic and all the way through my first full draft, Matt Trinetti, Parul Bavishi, Lauren Deborah, and other hosts of The Writers Hour saw me through countless marathon work sessions. The Faculty Write groups at Duke University and their rhizomatic offshoots have provided consistent camaraderie, too. Group leaders Melissa Simmermeyer, Sandra Valnes Quammen, Tolly Boatwright, and Erika Weiberg have all held space for writing, which we could not have done without Jennifer Ahern-Dodson's leadership and advocacy. During a critical stage, weekly writing meetings with Jennifer and Althea Portier-Young, Stephanie Norander, and Monique Dufour buoyed me beyond measure. My UB colleague Nicole Morris Johnson joined me for the homestretch, urging me out of the office and into our sunny café to write together.

Mimi Herman has been hearing research stories, reading transcript poems, jumping up and down with me at high points, and strategizing with me at the low points for the duration. My longtime friends Anna Rita Napoleone and Lauren Rosenberg waded through the weediest drafts and encouraged me to do the gutsiest analysis and edits. Their influence is throughout.

Some of my thinking about participatory methodology appears in other publications, although the analysis is new for the book. Lauren Rosenberg and I discuss co-interpretation in two chapters in *Improvisations: Methods and Methodologies for Lifespan Writing Research* (2024). "Interpreting Research with Participants: A Lifespan Writing Methodology" develops the theory and lineage of this methodology. In "Co-Interpretation in Action," we demonstrate our practice with collaborators Gwen Porter McGowan and Adrienne Long. My article on faculty-student research collaborations, "Rethinking Research in English with Nontraditional Adult Students," appears in *Pedagogy* (2022). In "Writing on the Job: Authorship, Ethics, and Agency," for the *Adult and Higher Education Alliance Proceedings* (2023), I discuss selected cases that also inform chapter 4.

My editor, Peggy Solic, has championed this book from our earliest correspondence. To Peggy and the production and marketing team at Rutgers University Press and to the anonymous readers who provided invaluable feedback, thank you for expert guidance in moving this from manuscript to monograph.

My dear friends and family, especially Gwen Trumbull, Jonathan Fulford, Beryl Fulford, Jess Alvarez, Ashton Alvarez, Will Inscoe, Campbell Inscoe, Sean Doig, Amanda McMillan, Agnieszka McCort, Kevin Poole, Natalie Szymanski, Elizabeth Sullivan, and David Gianturco, have all been understanding about the gravitational pull of this project—up to a point. They never let me go too long without restorative meals, walks, talks, and adventures. Finally, my spouse and favorite human on the planet, Becky Trumbull, held everything together for us for many years so I could write. Thank you.

Notes

Introduction

1 A pseudonym.

2 Stuart Parrish and most other students cited in this book have all requested use of their real names. Because of this, throughout the remainder of the book, endnotes indicate when I use a pseudonym instead.

Chapter 1 Confronting Ageism in Higher Education

1 Tressie McMillan Cottom's book, *Lower Ed*, documents the aggressive marketing, efficient onboarding, and financial aid machinery that accounts for the continued draw of private for-profit institutions like Strayer-NC for adult students. She also discusses the discrepancies between rising cultural expectations of "college for all" and the incommensurately small supply of higher-quality higher education that is accessible to marginalized populations.

2 More than half of the degree-seeking part-time students enrolled in the UNC system are over the age of twenty-five (Interactive Data Dashboards 2023).

3 Wings—Adult Education. Meredith College (website), https://web.archive.org/web/20231207164108/https://www.meredith.edu/adult-education.

Chapter 2 Doing Research about and with Adult Students

1 Both are pseudonyms.

Chapter 3 Rewriting Persistence

1 Oxford English Dictionary, s.v. "persist (v.)," September 2024, https://doi.org/10.1093/OED/3379341965.

2 When I met with Tamara in 2023 to review a version of this chapter, she told me she had also completed her master's in social work through an accelerated one-year program at the state flagship university.

3 North Carolina's higher education systems provide guidance to state institutions about credit for prior learning; however, assessment methods that could be used to evaluate informal and holistic learning such as Tamara's community authority are far less developed than standardized assessments such as subject-area CLEP tests. A 2023 revision to the North Carolina Community Colleges Curriculum Procedures Reference Manual lists portfolio assessment as one of six methods for awarding credit for prior learning. However, the section on portfolios is listed as "under development" (Curriculum Procedures 2023).

4 Adelman's report only tracks postsecondary students for eight and one-half years, however, as it is based on NCES data limited to that time span. The undergraduate histories of Tamara and many other participants in this book extend beyond that threshold.

5 *Encyclopedia Britannica Online*, s.v. "Merce Cunningham," last updated Apr 13, 2023, https://www.britannica.com/biography/Merce-Cunningham.

6 Excerpts from Tamara's personal preparatory notes are faithful to the original writing. This includes maintaining lowercase "black," which is otherwise capitalized in this book. The intended reader for these notes was only Tamara, who referred to them during her speech. Wording during the speech may have differed.

Chapter 4 Writers at Work

1 A pseudonym.

2 A self-selected pseudonym.

3 This interview took place during the COVID-19 pandemic.

4 Kenton worked in business finance prior to his career in health care.

5 Because their educational histories inform their professional perspectives on higher education, I include more biographical information about these three participants than others in this chapter.

6 A self-selected pseudonym.

Chapter 5 Writing with Emotion

1 A pseudonym.

2 A pseudonym.

Conclusion

1 See Stephan Johnson,"68-Year-Old Woman Graduates, Named Valedictorian at Kentucky's HBCU After Growing Up in Segregation," *WDRB.com,* May 17, 2023.

2 See Melissa Noel, "101-Year-Old Woman Returned to School and Will Graduate College with Her Granddaughter," *Essence*, January 24, 2024.

3 See "Mother Gets Pregnant at 13; Her Son Dropped Out of High School at 16, Both get PHDs at the Same Time," *Images You Won't See on T.V.*, March 14, 2024.

References

Adelman, Clifford. 2006. *The Toolbox Revisited: Paths to Degree Completion from High School Through College*. Washington, DC: U.S. Department of Education. https://www2.ed.gov/rschstat/research/pubs/toolboxrevisit/toolbox.pdf.

Ahmed, Sara. 2014. *The Cultural Politics of Emotion*. 2nd ed. Edinburgh, UK: Edinburgh University Press.

Alvarez, Angelica. 2017. "Durham Elementary School Facing Unprecedented State Takeover." *ABC 11 Eyewitness News*, October 11, 2017. https://abc11.com/durham-public-schools-glenn-elementary-school-charter-underperforming/2517789/.

Amundsen, Diana. 2022. "Life Is Not Always Linear: Expanding the Notion of Transitions in Higher Education to Challenge Structural, Static and Linear Processes Facing Indigenous and Older Adult Students." *Studies in Higher Education* 47, no. 8: 1681–1693. https://doi.org/10.1080/03075079.2021.1948526.

Arnette, Autumn A. 2015. "Funding at HBCUs Continues to be Separate and Unequal." *Diverse Issues in Higher Education,* March 31, 2015. http://diverseeducation.com/article/73463/.

Babb, Stephanie. 2022. *Meeting the Needs of Nontraditional Undergraduate Students*. Hershey, PA: IG Global.

Balay, Anne. 2018. *Semi Queer: Inside the World of Gay, Trans, and Black Truck Drivers*. Chapel Hill: The University of North Carolina Press.

Barton, David. 2009. "Researching Adult Learners' Lives to Understand Engagement and Progression in Learning." *Literacy & Numeracy Studies* 17, no. 1 (October): 51–61, https://doi.org/10.5130/lns.v0i0.1277.

Berg, B., S. Lee, B. Randolph, M. Ryu, and D. Shapiro. May 2023. *Current Term Enrollment Estimates: Spring 2023*. Herndon, VA: National Student Clearinghouse Research Center.

Blaauw-Hara, Mark. 2021. *From Military to Academy: The Writing and Learning Transitions of Student-Veterans*. Logan: Utah State University Press.

Blumenstyk, Goldie. 2018. *The Adult Student: The Population Colleges—and the Nation—Can't Afford to Ignore*. Washington, DC: The Chronicle of Higher Education.

Boland, William Casey and Marybeth Gasman. 2014. *America's Public HBCUs: A Four State Comparison of Institutional Capacity and State Funding Priorities*. Philadelphia: Penn Center for Minority Serving Institutions.

Bowl, Marion, and Ann-Marie Bathmaker. 2016. "'Non-traditional' Students and Diversity in Higher Education." In *The Routledge Handbook of the Sociology of Higher Education*, edited by James E Côté and Andy Furlong, 142–152. London, UK: Routledge.
Brandt, Deborah. 2015. *The Rise of Writing: Redefining Mass Literacy.* Cambridge: Cambridge University Press.
Browdy, Ronisha. 2021. "Black Women's Rhetoric(s): A Conversation Starter for Naming and Claiming a Field of Study." *Peitho* 23, no. 4 (Summer).
Bunch, Kay Jernigan and Palladi, Rhonda. 2017. "Assumptions about Older Faculty and the Quality of Higher Education." *Academy of Management Annual Meeting Proceedings*. Briarcliff Manor, NY: Academy of Management. https://doi.org/10.5465/AMBPP.2017.11401abstract.
Byrd, W. Carson, Rachelle J. Brunn-Bevel, and Sarah M. Ovink, eds. 2019. *Intersectionality and Higher Education: Identity and Inequality on College Campuses*. New Brunswick, NJ: Rutgers University Press.
Carey, Tamika L. 2020. "Necessary Adjustments: Black Women's Rhetorical Impatience." *Rhetoric Review* 39, no. 3 (September): 269–286. https://doi.org/10.1080/07350198.2020.1764745.
Carnegie Classification of Institutions of Higher Education. 2023. American Council on Education. https://carnegieclassifications.acenet.edu/.
Carroll, Lee Ann. 2002. *Rehearsing New Roles: How College Students Develop as Writers*. Carbondale: Southern Illinois University Press.
Cataldi, Emily Forrest, Christopher T. Bennett, and Xianglei Chen. 2018. *First-Generation Students: College Access, Persistence, and Postbachelor's Outcomes.* National Center for Education Statistics. Washington, DC: U.S. Department of Education.
Causey, Jennifer, Allyson Gardner, Aaron Pevitz, Mikyung Ryu, and Doug Shapiro. 2023. *Some College, No Credential Student Outcomes: Annual Progress Report—Academic Year 2021/22*. Herndon, VA: National Student Clearinghouse Research Center. https://nscresearchcenter.org/wp-content/uploads/SCNCReport2023.pdf.
Chen, Jin, Mary B. Ziskin, and Vasti Torres. 2020. "An Analysis of Factors Affecting Dropout Risks of Nontraditional Students: Evidence from U.S. 4-Year Commuter Institutions." *International Journal of Education Reform* 29, no. 1: 38–59. https://doi.org/10.1177/1056787919874864.
Childress, Greg. 2017. "Durham School Escapes Possible State Takeover. Parent Calls Decision 'a Win-Win'." *The Herald Sun*, October 13, 2017. https://www.heraldsun.com/news/local/education/article178701176.html.
Cohen, Alison K., Sarah Ryan, Louisa H. Smith, Robert K. Ream, M. Maria Glymour, Andrea Lopez, and Irene H. Yen. 2022. "Educational Attainment Past the Traditional Age of Completion for Two Cohorts of US Adults: Inequalities by Gender and Race/Ethnicity." *Race and Social Problems* 14, no. 3 (September): 208–222. https://doi.org/10.1007/s12522-021-09352-1.
Collins, Patricia Hill. 2019. *Intersectionality as Critical Social Theory.* Durham, NC: Duke University Press.
———. 2000. *Black Feminist Thought: Knowledge, Consciousness, and the Politics of Empowerment.* 2nd ed. New York: Routledge.
Crisp, Gloria, Catherine L. Horn, Margaret Kuczynski, Qiong Zhou, and Elizabeth Cook. 2019. "Describing and Differentiating Four-Year Broad Access Institutions:

An Empirical Typology." *The Review of Higher Education* 42, no 4: 1373–1400. https://doi.org/10.1353/rhe.2019.0069.

Curriculum Procedures Reference Manual: Credit for Prior Learning. 2023. North Carolina Community Colleges (website). https://wordpress.nccommunitycolleges.edu/wp-content/uploads/2024/01/Section19_19Dec2023_Credit-for-Prior-Learning.pdf.

Deleuze, Gilles, and Félix Guattari. 1988. *A Thousand Plateaus: Capitalism and Schizophrenia*. London: The Athlone Press.

Dippre, Ryan J., and Talinn Phillips. 2024. "Radicality in the Short Term: Generating Structural Change," in *Improvisations: Methods and Methodologies for Lifespan Writing Research,* edited by Ryan Dippre and Talinn Phillips, 373–382. Denver: WAC Clearinghouse/University Press of Colorado. https://doi.org/10.37514/PER-B.2024.2289.2.21.

Doe, Sue, and Lisa Langstraat, eds. 2014. *Generation Vet: Composition, Student Veterans, and the Post-9/11 University.* Logan: Utah State University Press.

Donaldson, Joe F., and Barbara K. Townsend. 2007. "Higher Education Journals' Discourse about Adult Undergraduate Students." *The Journal of Higher Education* 78, no. 1 (January/February): 27–50. https://doi.org/10.1080/00221546.2007.11778962.

Edbauer Rice, Jenny. 2008. "The New 'New': Making a Case for Critical Affect Studies." *The Quarterly Journal of Speech* 94, no. 2 (May): 200–212. https://doi.org/10.1080/00335630801975434.Edwards, Mike, and Alexis Hart, eds. 2010. "Logging On: Special Issue: Rhetoric, Technology, and the Military." *Kairos* 14, no. 3 (Summer).

Emig, Janet. 1977. "Writing as a Mode of Learning." *College Composition and Communication* 28, no. 2 (May): 122–128.

Faulkner, Sandra L. 2020. *Poetic Inquiry: Craft, Method and Practice.* 2nd ed. New York: Routledge.

Frigo, Stefanie, and Collie Fulford. Forthcoming. "Radical Adaptability: Research with Adult Learners." *Perspectives on Undergraduate Research and Mentoring.*

Fulford, Collie. 2019. "Subverting Austerity: Advancing Writing at a Historically Black University." *Pedagogy: Critical Approaches to Teaching Literature, Language, Composition, and Culture* 19, no. 2 (March): 225–241. https://doi.org/10.1215/15314200-7295900.

———. 2022. "Rethinking Research in English with Nontraditional Adult Students." *Pedagogy: Critical Approaches to Teaching Literature, Language, Composition, and Culture* 22, no. 1 (January): 79–98. https://doi.org/10.1215/15314200-9385488.

———. 2023. "Writing on the Job: Authorship, Ethics, and Agency." In *Workforce Development: Micro-Credentials, Badges, and CEUs. Adult and Higher Education Alliance Proceedings, 47th Annual Conference,* edited by Patricia Coberly-Holt and Kemmi Elufiede, 26–34. Minneola, FL: Adult Higher Education Alliance.

Fulford, Collie, and Lauren Rosenberg. 2024. "Interpreting Research with Participants: A Lifespan Writing Methodology." In *Improvisations: Methods and Methodologies for Lifespan Writing Research,* edited by Ryan Dippre and Talinn Phillips, 87–101. Denver: WAC Clearinghouse/University Press of Colorado. https://doi.org/10.37514/PER-B.2024.2289.2.05.

Gardner, Alyson. 2022. *Persistence and Retention Fall 2020 Beginning Postsecondary Student Cohort.* Herndon, VA: National Student Clearinghouse Research Center.

Gawande, Atul. 2010. *The Checklist Manifesto: How to Get Things Right*. New York: Metropolitan Books.

Geisler, Cheryl, and Jason Swartz. 2019. *Coding Streams of Language: Techniques for the Systematic Coding of Text, Talk, and Other Verbal Data*. Fort Collins: WAC Clearinghouse/University Press of Colorado.

Gerger, Heike, Christoph Patrick Werner, Jens Gaab, and Pim Cuijpers. 2021. "Comparative Efficacy and Acceptability of Expressive Writing Treatments Compared with Psychotherapy, Other Writing Treatments, and Waiting List Control for Adult Trauma Survivors: A Systematic Review and Network Meta-Analysis." *Psychological Medicine* 52, no. 15 (February): 3484–3496. https://doi.org/10.1017/S0033291721000143.

Glass, Oliver, Mark Dreusicke, John Evans, Elizabeth Bechard, and Ruth Q. Wolever. 2019. "Expressive Writing to Improve Resilience to Trauma: A Clinical Feasibility Trial." *Complementary Therapies in Clinical Practice* 34 (February): 240–246. https://doi.org/10.1016/j.ctcp.2018.12.005.

Global Report on Ageism. 2021. Geneva: World Health Organization.

Goldblatt, Eli. 2017. "Don't Call It Expressivism: Legacies of a 'Tacit Tradition.'" *College Composition and Communication* 68, no. 3 (February): 438–465. https://doi.org/10.58680/ccc201728962.

Gravett, Karen. 2021. "Troubling Transitions and Celebrating Becomings: From Pathway to Rhizome." *Studies in Higher Education* 46, no. 8: 1506–1517. https://doi.org/10.1080/03075079.2019.1691162.

Grawe, Nathan D. 2018. *Demographics and the Demand for Higher Education*. Baltimore, MD: Johns Hopkins University Press.

Guo, Lin. 2023. "The Delayed, Durable Effect of Expressive Writing on Depression, Anxiety and Stress: A Meta-analytic Review of Studies with Long-term Follow-ups." *British Journal of Clinical Psychology* 62, no. 1 (March): 272–297. https://doi.org/10.1111/bjc.12408.

Hart, Alexis D., and Roger Thompson. 2020. *Writing Programs, Veterans Studies, and the Post-9/11 University: A Field Guide*. Urbana, IL: Conference on College Composition and Communication/National Council of Teachers of English.

Hassel, Holly. 2022. "2022 CCC Chair's Address: Writing (Studies) and Reality: Taking Stock of Labor, Equity, and Access in the Field." *College Composition and Communication* 74, no. 2 (December): 208–228.

Hassel, Holly, and Cassandra Phillips. 2022. *Materiality and Writing Studies: Aligning Labor, Scholarship, and Teaching*. Urbana, IL: Conference on College Composition and Communication/National Council of Teachers of English.

Hendrix, Katherine Grace. 2021. "There Are No Awards for Surviving Racism, Sexism, and Ageism in the Academy: Contemplations of a Senior Faculty Member." *Communication and Critical/Cultural Studies* 18, no. 3: 246–262. https://doi.org/10.1080/14791420.2020.1865551.

Hernandez, Ayana. 2013. "North Carolina Central University Chancellor Debra Saunders-White Takes Office," press release, PRWeb, June 7, 2013. https://www.prweb.com/releases/2013/6/prweb10808536.htm.

Herrington, Anne J., and Marcia Curtis. 2000. *Persons in Process: Four Stories of Writing and Personal Development in College*. Urbana, IL: National Council of Teachers of English.

Hökkä, Päivi Kristiina, Eija Räikkönen, Heini Ikävalko, Susanna Paloniemi, and Katja Vähäsantanen. 2022. "Emotional Agency at Work: The Development and Validation of a Measure." *Frontiers in Education* 7 (July): 1–16. https://doi.org/10.3389/feduc.2022.852598.

hooks, bell. 1994. *Teaching to Transgress: Education as the Practice of Freedom*. New York: Routledge.

———. 2000. *Black Feminist Theory: From Margin to Center.* 2nd ed. Cambridge, MA: South End Press Classics.

———. 2015. *Yearning: Race, Gender, and Cultural Politics*. 2nd ed. New York: Routledge.

Horn, Laura J., and C. Dennis Carroll. 1996. *Nontraditional Undergraduates: Trends in Enrollment from 1986 to 1992 and Persistence and Attainment Among 1989–1990 Beginning Postsecondary Students.* Washington, DC: U.S. Department of Education, National Center for Educational Statistics.

Hui, T. Keung, and Greg Childress. 2017. "NC Narrows List of Schools Under Consideration for State Takeover." *The News and Observer*, October 4, 2017. https://www.newsobserver.com/news/local/education/article177028116.html.

Interactive Data Dashboards: Enrollment. 2023. University of North Carolina System (website). https://www.northcarolina.edu/impact/stats-data-reports/interactive-data-dashboards/.

IPEDS (Integrated Postsecondary Data System) n.d. Data Tools: Compare Institutions (website). U.S. Department of Education, Institute of Education Sciences, National Center for Educational Statistics. https://nces.ed.gov/ipeds/use-the-data.

Ivaniĉ, Roz. 1998. *Writing and Identity: The Discoursal Construction of Identity in Academic Writing.* Philadelphia: John Benjamins.

Iverson, Susan V. 2014. "Identity Constellations: An Intersectional Analysis of Female Student Veterans." In *Intersectionality and Higher Education: Theory, Research, and Praxis,* edited by Donald Mitchell, Charlana Simmons, and Lindsay Greyerbiehl, 135–145. New York: Peter Lang.

Jensen, Darin, and Brett Griffiths, eds. 2023. *Two-Year College Writing Studies: Rationale and Praxis for Just Teaching.* Logan: Utah State University Press.

Jiang, Jialei. 2024. "Composing to Enact Affective Agency: Engaging Multimodal Antiracist Pedagogy in the First-Year Writing Classroom." *Composition and Communication* 75, no. 3 (February): 534–557.

Johnson, Peggy. 2021. "Through a Glass, Darkly: The Hidden Injury of Ageism in the Academy." *Academic Labor: Research and Artistry* 5, no. 1. https://digitalcommons.humboldt.edu/alra/vol5/iss1/5.

Kasworm, Carol. 2018. "Adult Students: A Confusing World in Undergraduate Higher Education. *The Journal of Continuing Higher Education*. 66, no. 2: 77–87. https://doi:10.1080/07377363.2018.1469077.

Krone, Kathleen J., and Debbie S. Dougherty. 2015. Re-claiming an Unfinished Past: From Emotional Labor to Critical Emotional Agency. *Electronic Journal of Communication* 25 (3). https://www.cios.org/ejcpublic/025/3/025302.html.

Lake, Peter F. 1999. "The Rise of Duty and the Fall of *In Loco Parentis* and other Protective Tort Doctrines in Higher Education Law." *Missouri Law Review* 64, no. 1 (Winter): article 6 1–28.

Lee, Philip. 2011. "The Curious Life of *In Loco Parentis* in American Universities." *Higher Education in Review* 8: 65–90.

Lorde, Audre. 1984. *Sister Outsider: Essays and Speeches*. Trumansburg, NY: Crossing Press.

Lunsford, Andrea A., Jenn Fishman, and Warren M. Liew. 2013. "College Writing, Identification, and the Production of Intellectual Property: Voices from the Stanford Study of Writing." *College English* 75, no. 5 (May): 470–492. https://doi.org/10.58680/ce201323563.

MacLure, Maggie. 2010. "The Offence of Theory." *Journal of Educational Policy*. 25, no. 2: 277–286. https://doi.org/10.1080/02680930903462316.

———. 2013. "Classification or Wonder? Coding as an Analytic Practice in Qualitative Research." In *Deleuze and Research Methodologies*, edited by Rebecca Coleman and Jessica Ringrose, 164–183. Edinburgh, UK: Edinburgh University Press.

———. 2022. "Resistance, Desistance: Bad Girls of Post-Qualitative Inquiry." *International Journal of Qualitative Studies in Education* 37, no. 3: 631–641. https://doi.org/10.1080/09518398.2022.2127025.

Mallory, Angie, and Doug Downs. 2014. "Uniform Meets Rhetoric: Excellence through Interaction." In *Generation Vet: Composition, Student Veterans, and the Post-9/11 University*, edited by Sue Doe and Lisa Langstraat, 51–72. Logan: Utah State University Press.

McMillan Cottom, Tressie. 2017. *Lower Ed: The Troubling Rise of For-Profit Colleges in the New Economy*. New York: The New Press.

Micciche, Laura R. 2005. "Emotions, Ethics, and Rhetorical Action." *JAC* 25, no. 1: 161–184. https://www.jstor.org/stable/20866681.

———. 2007. *Doing Emotion: Rhetoric, Writing, Teaching*. Portsmouth, NH: Boynton/Cook.

———. 2016. "Staying with Emotion." *Composition Forum* 34 (Summer). https://compositionforum.com/issue/34/micciche-retrospective.php.

Michaud, Michael. 2013. "Literacy in the Lives of Adult Students Pursuing Bachelor's Degrees." *Open Words* 7 (Spring): 72–95. https://doi.org/10.37514/OPW-J.2013.7.1.06.

Miller, Elizabeth Ellis, Cameron Mozafari, Justin Lohr, and Jessica Enoch. 2023. "Thinking about Feeling: The Roles of Emotion in Reflective Writing." *College Composition and Communication* 74, no. 3 (February): 485–521. https://doi.org/10.58680/ccc202332364.

Mitchell, Donald, Charlana Simmons, and Lindsay Greyerbiehl, eds. 2014. *Intersectionality and Higher Education: Theory, Research, and Praxis*. New York: Peter Lang.

Montes, Soledad and Karen Tusting. 2024. "Writing in Transitions Across the Lifespan." In *Improvisations: Methods and Methodologies for Lifespan Writing Research*, edited by Ryan Dippre and Talinn Phillips, 231–247. Denver: WAC Clearinghouse/University Press of Colorado. https://doi.org/10.37514/PER-B.2024.2289.2.13.

Morrow-Howell, Nancy, Natalie Galucia, Emma Swinford, and Tanner Meyer. 2022. "Challenges and Opportunities of Age Diverse Universities: Perspectives from Admissions and Career Services." *Gerontology & Geriatrics Education* 43, no. 3 (July–September): 328–45. https://doi.org:10.1080/02701960.2020.1864345.

NCES (National Center for Education Statistics). 2015. *Demographic and Enrollment Characteristics of Nontraditional Undergraduates: 2011–12*. Washington, DC: U.S. Department of Education. https://nces.ed.gov/pubs2015/2015025.pdf.

———. 2021. "Table 303.50. Total Fall Enrollment in Degree-Granting Postsecondary Institutions, by Level of Enrollment, Control and Level of Institution, Attendance Status, and Age of Student: 2019." *Digest of Educational Statistics: 2021*. Washington, DC: U.S. Department of Education. https://nces.ed.gov/programs/digest/d21/tables/dt21_303.50.asp.

———. 2022a. "Table 306.10: Total Fall Enrollment in Degree-granting Postsecondary Institutions, by Level of Enrollment, Sex, Attendance Status, and Race/Ethnicity or Nonresident Status of Student: Selected Years, 1976 through 2021." *Digest of Educational Statistics*. Washington, DC: U.S. Department of Education.

———. 2022b. "Undergraduate Retention and Graduation Rates." *Condition of Education*. Washington, DC: U.S. Department of Education, Institute of Education Sciences. https://nces.ed.gov/programs/coe/indicator/ctr.

———. 2023. "Postsecondary Institution Expenses." *Condition of Education*. Washington, DC: U.S. Department of Education.

NSCRC (National Student Clearinghouse Research Center). 2023. *Persistence: Assessing Equity Gaps in Persistence*. DEI Data Lab. Herndon, VA: National Student Clearinghouse. https://www.studentclearinghouse.org/dei-data-lab/research-data/persistence-data/.

Ohito, Esther O., and Tiffany M. Nyachae. 2019. "Poetically Poking at Language and Power: Using Black Feminist Poetry to Conduct Rigorous Feminist Critical Discourse Analysis." *Qualitative Inquiry* 25, nos. 9–10: 839–850. https://doi-org/10.1177/1077800418786303.

Patel, Vimal. 2019. "The New 'In Loco Parentis.'" *Chronicle of Higher Education*. February 17, 2019.

Pearson, A. Fiona. 2019. *Back in School: How Student Parents are Transforming College and Family*. New Brunswick, NJ: Rutgers University Press.

Pearson, Walter. 2019. "Persistence of Adult Students." *The Journal of Continuing Higher Education* 67, no. 1: 13–23. https://doi:10.1080/07377363.2019.1627166.

Philip, Lisa. 2017a. "After Parent and Educator Opposition, State Removes Durham School from Takeover List." *WUNC North Carolina Public Radio*, October 13, 2017. https://www.wunc.org/education/2017-10-13/after-parent-and-educator-opposition-state-removes-durham-school-from-takeover-list.

———. 2017b. "Durham Parents Feel 'Taken Over' by School Takeover Process." *WUNC North Carolina Public Radio*, October 2, 2017. https://www.wunc.org/education/2017-10-02/durham-parents-feel-taken-over-by-school-takeover-process.

Phillips, Talinn, and Ryan Dippre. 2024. "Conducting Lifespan Writing Research: Challenges, Opportunities, and the State of a Radical Research Agenda." In *Improvisations: Methods and Methodologies for Lifespan Writing Research*, edited by Ryan Dippre and Talinn Phillips, 3–9. Denver: WAC Clearinghouse/University Press of Colorado. https://doi.org/10.37514/PER-B.2024.2289.1.3.

Pierpont, Darlene. 2020. "Potential: Student Perspective." In *Sixteen Teachers Teaching: Two-Year College Perspectives*, edited by Patrick Sullivan, 125–126. Logan: Utah State University Press.

Price, Margaret, and Stephanie L. Kerschbaum. 2016. "Stories of Methodology: Interviewing Sideways, Crooked and Crip." *Canadian Journal of Disability Studies* 5, no. 3 (October): 18–53. https://doi.org/10.15353/cjds.v5i3.295.

Ratcliff, Krista. 2005. *Rhetorical Listening: Identification, Gender, Whiteness*. Carbondale: Southern Illinois University Press.

Reichert Powell, Pegeen. 2013. *Retention and Resistance: Writing Instruction and Students Who Leave*. Boulder: University Press of Colorado.

Reinhold, Maren, Paul-Christian Bürkner, and Heinz Holling. 2018. "Effects of Expressive Writing on Depressive Symptoms—A Meta-analysis." *Clinical Psychology* 25, no. 1: e12224–n/a.

Reynolds, Tracey. 2002. "Re-Thinking a Black Feminist Standpoint." *Ethnic and Racial Studies* 25, no. 4 (December): 591–606. https://doi.org/10.1080/01419870220136709.

Richardson, Elaine B. 2013. *PHD to Ph. D: How Education Saved My Life*. Philadelphia: New City Community.

Rodriguez, Kevin. 2020. "Mindfulness: Student Perspective." In *Sixteen Teachers Teaching: Two-Year College Perspectives*, edited by Patrick Sullivan, 127–130. Logan: Utah State University Press.

Roozen, Kevin, and Erickson, Joe. 2017. *Expanding Literate Landscapes: Persons, Practices, and Sociohistoric Perspectives of Disciplinary Development*. Logan: Computers and Composition Digital Press/Utah State University Press. http://ccdigitalpress.org/expanding/.

Roozen, Kevin, and Karen J. Lunsford. 2011. "'One Story of Many to Be Told': Following Empirical Studies of College and Adult Writing through 100 Years of NCTE Journals." *Research in the Teaching of English* 46, no. 2: 193–209. https://doi.org/10.58680/rte201118266.

Rose, Mike. 1989. *Lives on the Boundary: The Struggles and Achievements of America's Underprepared*. New York: Free Press.

Rosenberg, Lauren. 2015. *The Desire for Literacy: Writing in the Lives of Adult Learners*. Urbana, IL: National Council of Teachers of English.

Rosenberg, Lauren, Collie Fulford, Gwen Porter McGowan, and Adrienne Long. 2024. "Co-Interpretation in Action." In *Improvisations: Methods and Methodologies for Lifespan Writing Research*, edited by Ryan Dippre and Talinn Phillips, 103–119. Denver: WAC Clearinghouse/University Press of Colorado. https://doi.org/10.37514/PER-B.2024.2289.2.06.

Royster, Jacqueline Jones. 1996. "When the First Voice You Hear Is Not Your Own." *College Composition and Communication* 47, no. 1 (February): 29–40. https://doi.org/10.2307/358272.

Ruini, Chiara, and Cristina C. Mortara. 2022. "Writing Technique Across Psychotherapies—From Traditional Expressive Writing to New Positive Psychology Interventions: A Narrative Review." *Journal of Contemporary Psychotherapy* 52 (September): 23–34. https://doi.org/10.1007/s10879-021-09520-9.

Schlemmer, Liz. 2022. "North Carolina's Experimental School Takeover Program Is Officially Ending This Summer." *WUNC North Carolina Public Radio*, April 11, 2022. https://www.wunc.org/news/2022-04-11/north-carolinas-experimental-school-takeover-program-is-officially-ending-this-summer.

Seidman, Irving. 2019. *Interviewing as Qualitative Research: A Guide for Researchers in Education and the Social Sciences*. 5th ed. New York: Teachers College Press.

Sekscenski, Lydia. 2020. "Encouragement: Student Perspective." In *Sixteen Teachers Teaching: Two-Year College Perspectives*, edited by Patrick Sullivan, 67–68. Logan: Utah State University Press.

Shapiro, D., M. Ryu, F. Huie, and Q. Liu. (October 2019), *Some College, No Degree, A 2019 Snapshot for the Nation and 50 States, Signature Report No. 17*. Herndon, VA: National Student Clearinghouse Research Center. https://nscresearchcenter.org/wp-content/uploads/SCND_Report_2019.pdf.

Shrider, Emily A., Melissa Kollar, Frances Chen, and Jessica Semega. 2021. *Income and Poverty in the United States: 2020. Report Number P60–273*. Washington, DC: United States Census Bureau.

Silverstein, Nina, Susan K. Whitbourne, Lauren M. Bowen, Joann M. Montepare, Taylor Jansen, Celeste Beaulieu, and Anya Prasad. 2022. "Assessing Age-Inclusivity in Higher Education: Introducing the Age-Friendly Inventory and Campus Climate Survey." *The Gerontologist* 62, no. 1 (February): e48–e61. https://doi.org/10.1093/geront/gnab090.

Simi, Demi, and Jonathan Matusitz. 2016. "Ageism Against Older U.S. College Students: A View from Social Closure Theory." *Interchange* 47, no. 4 (November): 391–408. https://doi.org/10.1007/s10780-016-9286-6.

Sissel, Peggy A., Catherine A. Hansman, and Carol E. Kasworm. 2001. "The Politics of Neglect: Adult Learners in Higher Education." *New Directions for Adult and Continuing Education* 91 (Fall): 17–28. https://doi.org/10.1002/ace.27.

Smalley, Suzanne. 2021. "UNC's $97 Million Plan to Reach Adult Online Learners." *Inside Higher Education*, December 8, 2021.

Smith, Christian Michael, Amber D. Villalobos, Laura T. Hamilton, and Charlie Eaton. 2023. "Promising or Predatory? Online Education in Non-Profit and For-Profit Universities." *Social Forces* (May): 1–26. https://doi.org/10.1093/sf/soad074.

Smitherman, Geneva. 1994. *Black Talk: Words and Phrases from the Hood to the Amen Corner.* Boston MA: Houghton Mifflin Company.

Soares, Louis, Jonathan S. Gagliardi, and Christopher J. Nellun. 2017. *The Post-Traditional Learners Manifesto Revisited: Aligning Postsecondary Education with Real Life for Adult Student Success.* Washington, DC: American Council on Education.

Sommers, Nancy. 1980. "Revision Strategies of Student Writers and Experienced Adult Writers." *College Composition and Communication* 31, no. 4 (December): 378–388. https://doi.org/10.2307/356588.

St. Pierre, Elizabeth Adams. 1997. "Methodology in the Fold and the Irruption of Transgressive Data." *International Journal of Qualitative Studies in Education*, 10, no. 2: 175–189. https://doi.org/10.1080/095183997237278.

Stenberg, Shari. 2015. *Repurposing Composition: Feminist Interventions for a Neoliberal Age.* Logan: Utah State University Press.

Stepule, Bridgette. 2020. "Flexibility: Student Perspective." In *Sixteen Teachers Teaching: Two-Year College Perspectives*, edited by Patrick Sullivan, 65–66. Logan: Utah State University Press.

Sternglass, Marilyn S. 1997. *Time to Know Them: A Longitudinal Study of Writing and Learning at the College Level.* New York: Routledge.

Strauss, Anselm, and Juliet Corbin. 1998. *Basics of Qualitative Research: Techniques and Procedures for Developing Grounded Theory.* 2nd ed. Thousand Oaks, CA: Sage.

Suh, Emily K. 2023. "Translating Habits of Persistence: Supporting Generation 1 Learners in Community College." In *Two-Year College Writing Studies: Rationales and Praxis for Just Teaching*, edited by Darin Jensen and Brett Griffiths, 61–78. Logan: Utah State University Press.

Suhr, M., A. K. Risch, and G. Wilz. 2017. "Maintaining Mental Health Through Positive Writing: Effects of a Resource Diary on Depression and Emotion Regulation." *Journal of Clinical Psychology* 73, no. 12 (December): 1586–1598. https://doi.org/10.1002/jclp.22463.

Sullivan, Patrick, ed. 2020. *Sixteen Teachers Teaching: Two-Year College Perspectives.* Logan: Utah State University Press.

Sullivan, Sherry E., and Akram Al Ariss. 2021. "Making Sense of Different Perspectives on Career Transitions: A Review and Agenda for Future Research." *Human Resource Management Review* 31, no. 1 (March): 100727. https://doi.org/10.1016/j.hrmr.2019.100727.

Sullivan, Sherry E., and Yehuda Baruch. 2009. "Advances in Career Theory and Research: A Critical Review and Agenda for Future Exploration." *Journal of Management* 35, no. 6: 1542–1571.

Sweat, Candace. 2017. "Durham Parents, Board Members Continue Fight Against Charter Takeover." *WRAL News*, October 11, 2017. https://www.wral.com/story/durham-parents-board-members-continue-fight-against-charter-takeover/17008133/.

Tarabochia, Sandra L. 2021. "From Resilience to Resistance: Repurposing Faculty Writers' Survival Strategies." *Peitho* 23, no. 3 (Spring).

———. 2024. "Becoming Researcher-Poets: Poetic Inquiry as Method/ology for Writing (through the Lifespan) Research." In *Improvisations: Methods and Methodologies for Lifespan Writing Research,* edited by Ryan Dippre and Talinn Phillips, 305–324. Denver: WAC Clearinghouse/University Press of Colorado. https://doi.org/10.37514/PER-B.2024.2289.2.17.

Taylor, Barrett J., and Brendan Cantwell. 2019. *Unequal Higher Education: Wealth, Status, and Student Opportunity.* New Brunswick, NJ: Rutgers University Press.

Taylor, Barrett J., Brendan Cantwell, Kimberly Watts, and Olivia Wood. 2020. "Partisanship, White Racial Resentment, and State Support for Higher Education." *The Journal of Higher Education* 91, no. 6: 858–887. https://doi.org/10.1080/00221546.2019.1706016.

Taylor, Carol A., and Jean Harris-Evans. 2018. "Reconceptualising Transition to Higher Education with Deleuze and Guattari." *Studies in Higher Education*, 43, no. 7: 1254–1267. https://doi.org/10.1080/03075079.2016.1242567.

Terenzini, Patrick T., and Ernest T. Pascarella. 1998. "Studying College Students in the 21st Century: Meeting New Challenges." *The Review of Higher Education* 21, no. 2 (Winter): 151–165. https://doi.org/10.1353/rhe.1998.a30045.

Thaiss, Christopher J., and Therese M. Zawacki. 2006. *Engaged Writers, Dynamic Disciplines: Research on the Academic Writing Life.* Portsmouth, NH: Heinemann.

The University of North Carolina System. 2017. *Higher Expectations: Strategic Plan for The University of North Carolina: 2017–2022.* https://www.northcarolina.edu/impact/strategic-plan/2017/.

Thelin, John R. 2019. *A History of Higher Education*. 3rd ed. Princeton, NJ: Princeton University Press.

Tinberg, Howard, and Jean-Paul Nadeau. 2010. *Community College Writer: Exceeding Expectations.* Carbondale: Southern Illinois University Press.

Tinto, Vincent. 2012. *Completing College: Rethinking Institutional Action*. Chicago: University of Chicago Press.

Turner, Jennifer, and Chaunté White. 2023. *Black Women Have Made Major Gains in Higher Education, but Black Single Mothers Still Struggle to Attain Degrees.* Washington, DC: Institute for Women's Policy Research.

UNC (University of North Carolina System). 2017. "UNC Initiative Aims to Help Former Students Earn Their Undergraduate Degrees." April 20, 2017. https://www.northcarolina.edu/news/approaching-the-finish-line/.

UNCGA (University of North Carolina General Administration). 2017. *Higher Expectations: Strategic Plan for the University of North Carolina—2017–2022.*

U.S. Bureau of Labor Statistics. 2015. "Number of Jobs Held, Labor Market Activity, and Earnings Growth Among the Youngest Baby Boomers: Results from a Longitudinal Survey." http://www.bls.gov/news.release/pdf/nlsoy.pdf.

U.S. Equal Employment Opportunity Commission. N.d. *Age Discrimination in Employment Act of 1967*. Washington, DC: U.S. Equal Employment Opportunity Commission. Accessed September 11, 2023, https://www.eeoc.gov/statutes/age-discrimination-employment-act-1967.

Villanueva, Victor. 1993. *Bootstraps: From an American Academic of Color.* Urbana, IL: National Council of Teachers of English.

Weenink, Don, and Gert Spaargaren, G. 2016. "Emotional Agency Navigates a World of Practices." In *Practice Theory and Research: Exploring the Dynamics of Social Life,* edited by Gert Spaargaren, Don Weenink, and Machiel Lamers, 60–84. New York: Routledge. https://doi.org/10.4324/9781315656908-14.

Wladis, Claire, Alyse C. Hachey, and Katherine Conway. 2023. "Time Poverty: A Hidden Factor Connecting Online Enrollment and College Outcomes?" *The Journal of Higher Education* 94, no. 4: 609–637. https://doi.org/10.1080/00221546.2022.2138385.

Wymer, Kathryn, Collie Fulford, Nia Baskerville, and Marisha Washington. 2012. "Necessity and the Unexpected: SoTL Student-Faculty Collaboration in Writing Program Research." *International Journal for the Scholarship of Teaching and Learning* 6, no. 1: Article 20, 1–7. https://doi.org/10.20429/ijsotl.2012.060120.

Yancey, Kathleen, ed. 2012. *A Rhetoric of Reflection*. Logan: Utah State University Press.

———. 1998. *Reflection in the Writing Classroom*. Logan: Utah State University Press.

Index

About the Author

COLLIE FULFORD is associate professor of English at the State University of New York at Buffalo.

Available titles in the American Campus series

Vicki L. Baker, Laura Gail Lunsford, and Meghan J. Pifer, *Developing Faculty in Liberal Arts Colleges: Aligning Individual Needs and Organizational Goals*

Derrick R. Brooms, Jelisa Clark, and Matthew Smith, *Empowering Men of Color on Campus: Building Student Community in Higher Education*

W. Carson Byrd, *Poison in the Ivy: Race Relations and the Reproduction of Inequality on Elite College Campuses*

Nolan L. Cabrera, *White Guys on Campus: Racism, White Immunity, and the Myth of "Post-Racial" Higher Education*

Adrianne Musu Davis, *Black and Smart: How Black High-Achieving Women Experience College*

Sherry L. Deckman, *Black Space: Negotiating Race, Diversity, and Belonging in the Ivory Tower*

Jillian M. Duquaine-Watson, *Mothering by Degrees: Single Mothers and the Pursuit of Postsecondary Education*

Scott Frickel, Mathieu Albert, and Barbara Prainsack, eds., *Investigating Interdisciplinary Collaboration: Theory and Practice across Disciplines*

Collie Fulford, *Insiders, Outliers: Centering Adult Student Writers at an HBCU*

Kirsten Hextrum, *Special Admission: How College Sports Recruitment Favors White Suburban Athletes*

Gordon Hutner and Feisal G. Mohamed, eds., *A New Deal for the Humanities: Liberal Arts and the Future of Public Higher Education*

Brandon A. Jackson, *Brotherhood University: Black Men's Friendships and the Transition to Adulthood*

Lisa Jasinski, *Stepping Away: Returning to the Faculty after Senior Academic Leadership*

Adrianna Kezar and Daniel Maxey, eds., *Envisioning the Faculty for the Twenty-First Century: Moving to a Mission-Oriented and Learner-Centered Model*

Ryan King-White, ed., *Sport and the Neoliberal University: Profit, Politics, and Pedagogy*

Yang Va Lor, *Unequal Choices: How Social Class Shapes Where High-Achieving Students Apply to College*

Dana M. Malone, *From Single to Serious: Relationships, Gender, and Sexuality on American Evangelical Campuses*

Z Nicolazzo, Alden Jones, and Sy Simms, *Digital Me: Trans Students Exploring Future Possible Selves Online*

Nathanael J. Okpych, *Climbing a Broken Ladder: Contributors of College Success for Youth in Foster Care*

A. Fiona Pearson, *Back in School: How Student Parents are Transforming College and Family*

Barrett J. Taylor and Brendan Cantwell, *Unequal Higher Education: Wealth, Status, and Student Opportunity*

James M. Thomas, *Diversity Regimes: Why Talk Is Not Enough to Fix Racial Inequality at Universities*